"Peace. Less. Still. Enough. S Uncluttered."

John Ortberg, senior pastor of Menlo Church, and author of I'd Like You More If You Were More Like Me

"Close the computer, put down the smartphone, grab a big cup of coffee and start reading this delightful and disorienting book. With disarming candor, sly humor, and the empathy of the pastor and spiritual counselor that she is, Courtney Ellis has given us a gift and offered us a path. Part intervention, part confession, part coaching, and part hanging-out-with-a-friend-that-makes-you-laugh-too-loud-in-a-restaurant, Ellis offers us a winsome, challenging, instructive, and inspiring engagement for rediscovering the freer, fuller life that all of us are longing for and most of us lost somewhere along the way."

Tod Bolsinger, Vice President & Chief of Leadership Formation, Fuller Seminary, and author of Canoeing the Mountains: Christian Leadership in Uncharted Territory

"Uncluttered is a practical and profound work, tailor-made for this era of noise and busyness. Courtney Ellis wisely and graciously points us to the secret of a fuller life, one that is slower and simpler, yet is more grounded and overflowing with the presence of a good and loving God."

Dorcas Cheng-Tozun, Inc.com columnist, and author of Start, Love, Repeat: How to Stay in Love with Your Entrepreneur in a Crazy Start-up World

"Uncluttered by Courtney Ellis is somehow raw, relatable, and hilarious, all at the same time. After reading the sentence, 'The light of Christ shines in through all of the new spaces created when we eliminate household clutter,' I dug up nine grocery bags of junk in less than a day—and truly felt a newfound sense of holiness and peace in the simplicity. I can't recommend her thoughts on decluttering the many different forms of clutter that fill up our lives more highly."

Cara Meredith, author of The Color of Life: A Journey toward Love and Racial Justice

WITHDRAWN

"One of the greatest threats to faith in the twenty-first century is distraction. The infinite access and limitless options of our age lead to lives of exhaustion, excess, and a 'too-muchness' where faith is just one among many consumer items we try to squeeze in. But this does not lead to flourishing. Key to healthy, sustainable, contagious faith is our commitment to living simpler, quieter, more uncluttered lives. This is the urgent and soul-nourishing message of Uncluttered, a book that should be read by anyone—pastors, parents, students, smartphone addicts—seeking to follow Jesus more attentively in an age of distraction."

Brett McCracken, senior editor for the Gospel Coalition, author of *Uncomfortable: The Awkward and Essential Challenge of Christian Community*

"In Uncluttered Rev. Courtney Ellis does what our time, image, and productivity obsessed culture tells us is impossible: unplugging from the unnecessary demands of life and instead plugging in to God and relationships that matter. With her profound spirituality, uncommon transparency, and gut-shaking humor (take off your shape wear before reading) she invites us to journey to a simpler, deeper, and stronger relationship with God, family, and work."

Nicole Caldwell-Gross, Pastor of Missions and Outreach at St. Luke's (UMC), and blogger

"Uncluttered is a funny, nonjudgmental, down-to-earth guide not just for clearing out junk, but for laying hold of freedom in order to perceive God and abide with him. With both humorous stories and ancient spiritual disciplines, Courtney Ellis walks alongside the reader with a true pastor's heart to discover the riches of an uncluttered life."

Aubry G. Smith, author of *Holy Labor: How Childbirth Shapes a Woman's Soul*

Uncluttered

Free Your Space,
Free Your Schedule,
Free Your Soul

Courtney Ellis

HENDRICKSON PUBLISHERS   ROSE PUBLISHING

Uncluttered
Rose Publishing, LLC
140 Summit Street
P.O. Box 3473
Peabody, Massachusetts 01961-3473
www.hendricksonrose.com

Book cover design by Nancy Bishop; page design by Nancy Bishop and Sergio Urquiza.

ISBN: 978-1-62862-791-6

Library of Congress Cataloging-in-Publication Data

Names: Ellis, Courtney (Courtney B.), author.
Title: Uncluttered : free your space, free your schedule, free your soul / by Courtney Ellis.
Description: Peabody, Massachusetts : Rose Publishing, [2019] | Includes bibliographical references.
Identifiers: LCCN 2018031360 (print) | LCCN 2018042211 (ebook) | ISBN 9781628628272 (ebook) | ISBN 9781628627916 (pbk.)
Subjects: LCSH: Simplicity--Religious aspects--Christianity.
Classification: LCC BV4647.S48 (ebook) | LCC BV4647.S48 E45 2019 (print) | DDC 241/.68--dc23
LC record available at https://lccn.loc.gov/2018031360

Printed in the United States of America
011018VP

To Daryl,
with all my heart

Contents

Part I
The Freedom of Less

Part II
The Grace of More

Why then, can one desire
too much of a good thing?

–Shakespeare, *As You Like It*, Act IV, Scene I

Part I

THE FREEDOM OF LESS

Introduction

I MIGHT DIE, BUT AT LEAST WE CAN AFFORD A SECOND CAR

We are all of us clinging to something.
–Scott Cairns, *The End of Suffering*

I sat in the academic building's hallway, a few doors down from the classroom in which I taught. I stared at the tan carpet, breathing in and out and trying with increasing desperation to will away an impending panic attack.

"Professor Ellis?"

I raised my gaze to the pair of ankle boots standing before me. "Yes?"

"Class started a couple of minutes ago," she said. One of my students. Hailey.

"Okay," I said. "I'll be right there." I waited for her to leave, took a few more breaths, and shakily got to my feet, heading down the hall for my final class of the day.

Get a grip, I told myself. *There's no reason you should be panicking.*

And really, there wasn't. It was a writing class, not the invasion of Fallujah.

Besides, the rest of my life was much too rosy for panic. In the past year, my husband Daryl and I celebrated the birth of our second son, a finished PhD (his), and a new blog (mine). Our marriage rocked: we were one of those annoying couples who both loved and liked each other. We lived in southern California where it was sunny pretty much every freaking day. We worked alongside each other at a thriving church with a fantastic staff.

So *why* exactly was I having a panic attack in a college hallway?

I confessed my ongoing anxiety to our Bible study small group a few days later. "It's all just too much," I told them, three other husband-and-wife duos who'd known me for years. "I'm overwhelmed all the time and it's all too much and I don't know how to make it less much."

"What exactly is too much?" my friend Eva asked.

"All of it," I said.

"Can you be more specific?" asked her husband.

"I *am being specific*!" I said.

Later the same night I sobbed in Daryl's arms and tried to put words to why I felt like I was drowning even though on the surface our life was nothing but great. I had no complaints at all, yet I couldn't breathe, struggled to sleep, and felt panicky nearly every second of every day. It didn't make sense. So together we began retracing our steps.

Slowly a picture came together. Over the course of our decade-long marriage, we'd gradually but continually stuffed more and more into our lives. Responsibilities, activities, vocations. Children, classes, cross-country moves. Small groups, Bible studies, mission trips, speaking engagements. In addition to all that, technology that barely existed when we'd first gotten married— Instagram, texting, mobile email—we now used regularly. We were totally connected, constantly available, and rapidly approaching burnout. I felt it most acutely, but Daryl was feeling it, too. His sleep

> WE WERE TOTALLY CONNECTED, CONSTANTLY AVAILABLE, AND RAPIDLY APPROACHING BURNOUT.

suffered; his joy diminished. He wore his exhaustion like a pair of smudged glasses—he could still see well enough, but nothing looked as sharp or clear or beautiful as it really was.

Then there was this particular year. We'd moved to southern California where our rent more than doubled for half the square footage of our Midwestern home. We welcomed our second-born, but having babies isn't free. To give Daryl the time he needed to complete his PhD, we relied on a babysitter more frequently. We still had a few student loans. Public transportation was spotty and unreliable, so we had to invest in a second car. We bought a used one (it was older than our marriage and in distinctly worse shape), but the costs still added up.

With all this on our plates, I'd done the logical thing and gotten a second job. We sailed along swimmingly. For a while.

With piles of papers to grade, I spent less time with Daryl and the kids. When he and I were together we were too spent to connect, so we'd numb out to television or fall asleep reading in bed. Our life together was cluttered.

We began allowing the preschooler to watch more and more TV, which made him cranky and irritable, but what could we do? Guilty about working so much, I'd bring home little toy surprises, which he'd quickly lose interest in after a day or two. His room was an overflowing, trinket-exploding mess, and he began acting out, hungry for more attention and less stuff. His life was cluttered.

Like most millennials, I spent all my waking hours tethered to my smartphone. My work boundaries were nonexistent, and often a last-minute tech check-in before bed would yield a fitful night of sleep after I discovered a conflictual email from a congregant or a late-night request from a student. My life was cluttered.

Often Daryl was only halfway present, glued to *Sports-Center* on a computer perched on a shelf above our crawling baby's reach. Finishing his PhD left him euphoric but limping, too. The road had been a long one. He scrolled through PhD job boards, updating his resume and obsessing over his chances of landing the perfect gig. His life was cluttered.

Even the baby, then only six months old, suffered from the too muchness of it all. I'd nurse him while responding to emails, noticing only occasionally that his little blue eyes were searching in vain to meet mine. His life was cluttered.

We were a hot mess, all of us, with me as the biggest offender of the Too Much Clan, always taking on more, saying yes, filling up time and space, wasting energy on little projects, teaching my brood to do likewise. Yet we persisted in our cluttered lives, unaware that there could possibly be another way.

We are sensible, my husband and I told ourselves. *We are frugal, thoughtful, wise people*, we told ourselves. *There's absolutely nothing we could do to make our life simpler!*

This simply wasn't true.

What *was* true was that it was too much. All of it. *Everything.* The schedule, the workload, the possessions, the technology, the wardrobe, the budget, the noise. The constant connectedness through email and social media and texting. The filled-to-the-brim calendar where we shoehorned so many houseguests into our tiny condo that our neighbors asked if we were secretly running a bed and breakfast. (Hey, you move to California from Wisconsin and people want to *visit*.)

It was all too much.

So...we stopped.

Not everything, and not all at once, but much of it. Most of it.

We had hard conversations and spent lots of time on our knees. We fought with God and sometimes each other, because giving up things is hard. We cancelled media subscriptions and pared down our mail. We subscribed to an honest-to-goodness newspaper, turned off cable, and stopped allowing ourselves to be consumed by the twenty-four-hour news cycle. We cleaned out our garage, our closets, our cabinets, our drawers. We took a *crapload* of stuff to Goodwill.

We said no a lot. No, thank you. No, really. No, not today, not tomorrow, not now, not ever.

We simplified our meals and wardrobes and schedules. We gave ourselves only ten minutes of mindless internet surfing a day, and then five. We deleted apps from our phones. First every social media app, and then almost everything else (more on that later).

Little by little the most amazing thing started to happen. We began to learn what was truly essential and what wasn't, and with each nonessential thing we let go of, our hearts grew calmer, quieter, more open, and more joyful. Our souls grew lighter. Our relationships grew deeper. And each and every time God pried our hands off of the things we clung to, he filled them anew with more of himself. It turns out that holding on to stuff and busyness was not grace but burden.

Slowly, God taught us to pray and read more deeply. To notice our kids: their moods, their needs, their sweet little faces. To help them slowly detox from a constant stream of activity and motion and technology and "educational television" and the latest Disney fad. We watched their little minds begin to sharpen and focus and rest and rejoice.

We *all* began to sleep better.

We started to see one another anew—the spouse we'd each fallen in love with all those years ago. We watched lines of exhaustion begin to fade, smiles begin to return, steps begin to slow, laughter begin to bubble up more easily and regularly.

The goodness we discovered went far beyond our own household. As we uncluttered, God taught us to grow more sensitive to our neighbors and our neighborhood, to the church calendar, to what was in season at the grocery store, to the nuances in the weather, and, most importantly, to the beautiful, subtle, powerful movement of the Holy Spirit in the world and the church, in our minds and in our midst.

WITH EACH NONESSENTIAL THING WE LET GO OF, OUR HEARTS GREW CALMER, QUIETER, MORE OPEN, AND MORE JOYFUL.

The more we gave up, the more we gained.

My panic? It stopped. Our budget? It became a thousand times easier to meet each month. Our trust in God? It grew exponentially. We aren't minimalists, but we have become minimal-ish, not just in our possessions but in our schedules, our home, our spending, and our souls.

Our goal was to find simplicity—not only because of its deep roots in Scripture, but because we wanted to find *ourselves* again. It turns out that God created and formed each of us for lives of generous simplicity; we only need to invite him in to help us make sense of our mess. Over time, the question for us changed from "How can we survive?" to "How can we let God arrange our lives, so we become the kind of people God created us to be?"

The answer became *Uncluttered*.

2

Stuff

MORE IS MORE, UNLESS IT'S NOT.

He who loves temporal things
loses the fruit of love.
–Clare of Assisi

We had so much crap.

I wasn't allowed to say *crap* as a kid. It was on the list of naughty words, along with *shut up* and *this sucks*. I grew up in a conservative, evangelical home. My middle sister didn't know the F-word existed until she read it off of a picnic table in junior high, much to my amusement and my mother's horror.

Yet every time my grandma came over for a visit, she'd head up the stairs to our bedrooms only to be greeted by piles of girl-child detritus. Barbies. My Little Ponies. Books. Dress-up clothes. Legos. Hockey sticks.

"Look at all this *crap*!" she'd exclaim.

"Moooooom," my two sisters and I would yell in unison, "how come Grandma can say *crap* and we can't?"

The thing was, a lot of it *was* crap. Tchotchkes from McDonald's Happy Meals. Bargain-bin finds from big-box stores. Made-in-China junk from the Dollar Tree. Eight thousand plastic, sparkly whatchamacallits from friends' birthday party goodie bags.

We had a few really wonderful, valuable toys. I was the proud owner of Samantha of American Girl Doll fame, and I cared for her like I was a lady-in-waiting to a medieval queen. Her hair was perfectly coiffed, her dress delicately pleated. She slept each night in her sturdy white box and if my sisters even thought about touching her, I'd scream.

But mostly we had a ton of crap. We spent lots of time cleaning it up. Organizing it. Reorganizing it. It was always a bit of a mess no matter how many bins or bookshelves my parents purchased to try to quell the overflow. My dad eventually stopped going upstairs to our bedrooms altogether. He just couldn't handle the pink plastic minefield.

Still, I didn't really understand how annoying kid mess could be until I had two of my own. Then I got it. Kid stuff multiplies at an incredible rate. I swear that our sons' toy cars get busy in the wee hours of the night because when I wake up there are *more of them*. Not to mention Christmas gifts. Birthday booty. That evil dollar bin at Target. The stuff adds up. And then it gets blessed *e'rywhere*.

Yet, to be honest, the adults in my house aren't much better. My husband loses half a dozen pens a week, so he buys new pens, and not just regular, normally priced pens, but *Le Pens* (yeah, that's really a thing), and then he finds the old *Le Pens* that he lost and suddenly we're drowning in these ridiculous, pretentious pens but when he's out at Starbucks working on a sermon he can't find one in his backpack so *he buys more pens*.

Not that I'm immune. I might not purchase small mountains' worth of writing utensils, but we live in southern California and I own nine jackets. Granted, we *used* to live in Wisconsin, but we don't anymore. Winter here is sixty degrees and sunny. But you know, *just in case*, I keep a giant white parka, a black pea coat, a black *full length* pea coat, a rust-colored autumn coat, a light fleece jacket, a heavier fleece jacket, a khaki trench coat, an old Mountain Hardware jacket from back when I used to be cool and go rock climbing in college, and a stupid raincoat that doesn't really even shed rain but *maybe someday I will waterproof it or something*. Right.

Here's the other thing: until very recently we lived in a two-bedroom condo. The four of us. The baby quite literally slept in a closet. So when we accumulated too much stuff, we couldn't even *breathe*. Cabinets wouldn't close. We tripped over stuff in the middle of the night. The entryway became Shoe Mountain.

I'd *had* it. I'd had it with the clutter, with the toys that never got put away, with Shoe Mountain, with the overflowing closets, with *Le Pens*. I needed a solution that didn't involve burning the whole place down and starting over, because I'm pretty sure arson should generally be off the table almost always.

Someone Get Me a Bulldozer

Oddly enough, I consider myself a natural purger. Most marriages have one saver and one thrower-outer, and I'm the one who tosses stuff. I am the least sentimental person on earth next to probably Donald Trump. Favorite shirt from college? If it doesn't fit anymore, it's going to Goodwill. Framed, autographed picture of Surya Bonaly? (I had an ice skating phase in the '90s. Don't judge.) Doesn't need to take up shelf space anymore. Kids' artwork? Meh. Take a picture of it and toss it in the garbage. (Some of you are now seriously doubt-

> I KNEW THAT THE COMFORT I RECEIVED FROM MY POSSESSIONS WAS FALSE COMFORT.

ing the state of my soul. But did you read the part about us living in a two-bedroom condo? Only takes a few big art projects before our home looks like we are auditioning for Hoarders.)

I'm not alone. Minimalism is making quite a comeback. From the tiny house movement to *Real Simple Magazine* to *The Minimalists Podcast* (tagline: "Less is Now!"), it turns out I wasn't the only one sick of my stuff running my life.

On a spiritual level, I knew that the comfort I received from my possessions was false comfort. Sure, a new shirt made me feel really good, but only for a day or two. Then I realized that I needed a new pair of pants to make the shirt really work. And that jamming another shirt into my overstuffed dresser drawer was annoying. And that salmon isn't really my color.

John Ortberg, in *The Life You've Always Wanted*, talks about making his first big furniture purchase: a really nice mauve sofa that he and his wife adored. Problem was, their kids were young, and kids are messy. So John and his wife made it clear to their kids what the new house rules were:

> Don't sit on the mauve sofa. Don't touch the mauve sofa. Don't play around the mauve sofa. Don't eat on, breathe on, look at, or think about the mauve sofa. Remember the forbidden tree in

the Garden of Eden? "On every other chair in the house you may freely sit, but upon this sofa, the mauve sofa, you may not sit, for in the day you sit thereupon, you shall surely die."[1]

It wasn't much fun in the Ortberg house once that sofa arrived. Then, of course, one of the kids stained it with jam, and after the initial brouhaha it went from being "the mauve sofa" to just another thing to sit on. Which is, by the way, why sofas exist in the first place.

Each of our possessions costs us not just money, but time, investment, and effort. The more stuff Daryl and I and our kids accumulated, the more dissatisfied I felt. It was like the possessions were crowding out my soul, taking up the space where my spirit wanted to grow. I wanted less stuff so I could have more *me*. More *us*. More *Jesus*. I just didn't know quite where to start.

Stuff Can't Save

Barbara Cawthorne Crafton, in an essay in *Bread and Wine*, asks how many possessions would ever be enough for our salvation. The answer, of course, is that possessions don't save. They can *never* save. But they could keep us so distracted we forgot the truth. "How did we come to know that we were dying a slow and unacknowledged death?" she writes, "And that the only way back to life was to set all our packages down and begin again, carrying with us only what we really needed?

"We travail. We are heavy laden. Refresh us, O homeless, jobless, possession-less Savior. You came naked, and naked you go. And so it is for us. So it is for all of us."[2] A haunting reminder when we feel that somehow, deep down, holding on to things will protect us from every eventuality, keep us safe, grant us immortality. (This is obviously silly. But I kind of believed it. Maybe you do, too.) Our trust cannot be in things.

> THE POSSESSIONS WERE CROWDING OUT MY SOUL, TAKING UP THE SPACE WHERE MY SPIRIT WANTED TO GROW.

Our safety and security must not be rooted in them. They don't, can't, *won't* last. Saving every piece of our children's artwork won't keep them young. Making sure we have the very best furniture won't strengthen our marriage. Buying the newest kitchen gadget won't help us love our neighbors better. (Unless that gadget is a self-cleaning kitchen robot, in which case *count me in.*) Cars, houses, toys, clothing—they rust, age, break, and go out of style. "Store up treasure in heaven," Jesus tells the crowds who've followed him up the mountain, "because where your treasure is, your heart will be there also."[3]

Southern California is home to a huge luxury car market. Makes and models of cars I'd never heard of before are commonplace on the freeways here. Maserati. Lamborghini. Aston Martin. There's a fancy mall near where we live that reserves a few parking spaces out front for these top-notch, crazy-expensive vehicles. My four-year-old, ever the car nut, always wants to walk past them and ogle.

Any time we wander closer than ten feet from one of the cars, inevitably an official-looking dude will get out of the driver's seat and just stand there, eyeing us. The message is clear: "If you get your peanut-butter-and-jelly-fingers on this Bentley, there will be hell to pay."

Not only do these cars cost tens of thousands (if not hundreds of thousands) of dollars, but those who drive them have to hire a guard for them, too. Who really owns whom?

To live an uncluttered life, we must give up stuff. Not all of it, but much of it. Most of it. I can hear you protesting, because I spent a lot of time protesting, too. My conversations with God sounded something like this:

But I need all this stuff!

No, really, you don't.

I...I might need some of this stuff!

Of course you do. I made you. I know you need some stuff. You need chairs to sit on and pots to cook in and clothes to wear and books to read. Your kids need toys to play with and coats when it's cold. For work you need a phone and a car and a computer. But you don't need all of it. Not nearly all of it.

And, Courtney? It isn't making you happy. And it definitely isn't helping you follow me the ways I want you to.

Yeah. You're kind of right, God.

I usually am.

Oh, duh. Well then, how do I decide what to get rid of?

Get rid of what you know you can. Then get rid of a little bit more. It'll start to become clear. And don't be afraid—I'll be with you the whole time.

Bit by Bit

I started with the garage. Our one-car garage, filled almost to the brim by ride-on toys and family heirlooms, all of it saved from our Midwestern days when space was plentiful and I happily accepted friends' hand-me-downs and hunted for garage sale gems, because we never knew what we might need.

First on the docket was the most obvious item: my parents' old dining room table. The one that filled up nearly half the garage. The one I ate dinner at every night as a child. The one that made sense in a large, Midwestern dining room but had absolutely no place in a two-bedroom condo. We'd tried. It took up the entire dining room and half the living room. One babysitter asked when we were planning to host a banquet.

I listed it online, and a pastor's wife quickly messaged me.

"We need a table where we can throw big dinners for the church," she wrote. "This will be perfect! Thank you so much!"

The same table that burdened us by eating up space, remaining in our garage for nearly two years because I felt so much guilt over even the idea of getting rid of it (it was my MOTHER'S!), now provided a blessing to someone who not only needed it—she needed it for *ministry*. It was one of those, "Okay, God, I get it and I'm sorry," moments. This letting go of stuff thing? Turns out it felt *good*.

Soon clothes I didn't wear and cookie cutters I never used were off to Goodwill. A children's charity organization took our outgrown baby toys. A neighbor picked up our spare stroller. We put our DVD collection and a big bin of CDs on Craigslist for free and didn't look back.

Instead of deciding what I could bear to give away, I started thinking about what I needed to keep at all. Sure, giving away five T-shirts is admirable, unless you still have forty in your closet (which, I'm embarrassed to say, I did). I opened every cabinet; I looked in every drawer; I braved the trunk of the car and the shelves in the kids' rooms. I was ruthless.

With every possession that left *my* possession I felt a little bit lighter. Less anxious. More tethered to the central things of life: my Jesus, my kids, my husband, my vocation.

It wasn't always easy, of course. My mother has German heritage and Germans save everything. *Everything.* Even things that most people would decide could safely head to the trash bin. We *have* to keep these sixteen paintbrushes. Why? Just in case, I don't know, the apocalypse comes and sixteen of us need to paint something.

Frugality is a great thing. A virtue, even. Reusing what we have and not buying new. Saving what we need so we don't have to shop again next month, next season, next year. Yet the paralysis I felt to keep things *just in case* made purging things I didn't really need kind of tough. I had to break through the *just in case.*

Turns out that in my case, "just in case" was more about control and fear than it was about frugality. I didn't want to be stuck without proper cold-weather gear if suddenly southern California became a tundra. I genuinely believed I might fit into my high school jeans again. Don't we all?

The Minimalists talk helpfully about these "just in case" items. They believe the words *just in case* are the most dangerous in the English language.[4] I disagree there, as I believe "He's got a gun" and "Your sister's becoming a vegan, I need you to talk to her" are significantly more dangerous. But the Minimalists have a point. Their policy on "just in case" items—those you haven't used recently and aren't very likely to need anytime soon—is simple: if you *did* need it and you could get it in under twenty minutes for under twenty dollars, *get rid of it.*

That was the permission I needed. And oh, it was glorious.

The Freedom of Less

Less stuff means more freedom. Wouldn't you rather have the time and mental energy you use for caring for all the stuff you don't need...for something else? *Anything* else? Perhaps you could reclaim those hours for something *besides* washing and putting away your thirty-seven kitchen utensils? Is it possible one can opener, a couple of wooden spoons, and a pancake flipper can do all the jobs just fine? (Did you know you can actually whisk eggs with a *fork*? Totes true, I promise.)

Do you *really* need eight shelves of knick-knacks? (I'm pretty sure "knick-knack" is Yiddish for "crap.") Are you ever going to *do* all of those 1,500-piece puzzles, or is it possible a single one could entertain you on a rainy day just as well? Can't you get most books from a library, most Blu-rays on Netflix, most camping equipment from that friend who backpacks every weekend?

I began to discover that I could.

Granted, I'm the one in our marriage who is wired to love getting rid of stuff. I've always been this way. Not terribly nostalgic, not super attached to things. This is not true of Daryl. He gets attached to stuff. To the memories that attach themselves to that stuff. Sometimes I'm sympathetic. I understand that some of his PhD library is sentimental, even though he'll never read all of Augustine's works ever again. (Or if he does, I'll definitely be dead already, because watching him go through all of that once nearly killed me.) But the two-toned dress shoes from his *high school prom*?!? Yeah, I've been trying to dump those for years and he pulls them out of the Goodwill bin *every single time*.

But part of living uncluttered is starting with ourselves and letting the peace and happiness and love we experience in uncluttering speak to those with whom we live. There are moments to suggest and moments to bite our tongues. I've had to let the prom shoes go. (Or *stay*, as it were...)

We still have some crap. It's hard to live in twenty-first-century America any other way. But as we continue to slowly pare down and weed out and simplify, I'm finding that the light of Christ shines in through all of the new spaces created when we eliminate household clutter. Closets filled with skis and umbrellas and flip flops and wrapping paper won't save us, but Jesus is waiting to do that very thing.

> GOD HAS VERY LITTLE INTEREST IN OUR POSSESSIONS, EXCEPT TO REMIND US THAT THEY MUST NEVER BE OUR UTMOST CONCERN.

After all, God isn't a God of stuff. He has very little interest in our possessions, except to remind us that they must never be our utmost concern. Instead he cares for us—body, mind, and soul—and points us toward caring for our neighbors. The less stuff I have to manage, the more I can manage *that*.

Clothing

THE ONE THING MARK ZUCKERBERG AND I HAVE IN COMMON

One's travels should begin at home.
–Wendell Berry, *The Unsettling of America: Culture and Agriculture*

My friend Eric eats exactly the same thing for lunch every single day. A turkey sandwich on wheat bread with lettuce, cheese, and tomato. An apple on the side. He has done this every single day for over three decades.

If this sounds horrifically boring to you and your taste buds, I am totally with you. In a world with burritos and pho and filet mignon (not to mention gummy bears! helllllo!), how can eating the same thing every single day possibly be a good thing?

"It's one less decision to make," Eric says. The guy's a brilliant biologist with a sheaf of published articles about bacteria I can't even pronounce, so maybe he's on to something. By eliminating the clutter of decisions about lunch, he frees his mind to think more deeply about bacteria. Which, come to think of it, would probably make me lose my appetite altogether. But the point stands.

Have you heard of decision fatigue? It's almost certain you suffer from it sometimes, even if you aren't aware of it. Decision fatigue is the exhaustion that creeps in after we've had to make choice after choice in a given day. It's why you're much more likely to cheat on your diet late at night than you are in the morning. It's why so many couples get into fights in Ikea. It's why grocery stores put the candy up near the registers— by the time you check out, you've usually made so many decisions already that your willpower is at an all-time low.

Science writer John Tierney puts it this way:

> No matter how rational and high-minded you try to be, you can't make decision after decision without paying a biological price. It's different from ordinary physical fatigue—you're not consciously aware of being tired—but you're low on mental energy. The more choices you make throughout the day, the harder each one becomes for your brain.[5]

If you've ever gotten to the end of a particularly stressful day and wondered why you felt like you'd run a marathon even though you'd only been behind a desk or the wheel of a car, decision fatigue is the answer.

Eric's lunch, though boring, is also a little bit brilliant. In addition to being a biologist, Eric leads worship for his church. Each night he sits with his piano and goes over the order of music, practicing hymns, arranging choruses, and preparing for Sunday's service. Making fewer decisions in the morning helps him make more thoughtful decisions after the sun goes down.

Some of the leaders and shakers of the global economy avoid decision fatigue in a different way. What do Mark Zuckerberg, Cornel West, and Steve Jobs have in common, besides being brilliant visionary thinkers? They each wear a super simple, streamlined wardrobe.

Zuckerberg, billionaire though he is, wears a T-shirt and a gray hoodie to work almost every single day. Longtime Princeton professor Cornel West's standard wardrobe is a classy black three-piece suit and a perfectly starched white shirt. Apple guru Jobs consistently presented to billionaire investors wearing a pair of faded Levis, New Balance running shoes, and

> DECISION FATIGUE IS THE EXHAUSTION THAT CREEPS IN AFTER WE'VE HAD TO MAKE CHOICE AFTER CHOICE IN A GIVEN DAY.

a cheap mock-turtleneck from L.L. Bean. They each wear (or wore, in Jobs' case) a self-styled, carefully chosen uniform. One fewer decision every morning, freeing up brain space for creativity, innovation, and the higher-level choices involved in running a company or teaching a seminar.

In a way, I envy them. Think of all the time and energy and aggravation and stress they save by simply going to a closet full of the same clothes each day! Think of the closet clutter you could cut down if you didn't have to have five different washes of jeans in eleven different styles. (Cropped! High-rise! Skinny! Flared! Skinny flared! Flared cropped skinny! Editor's cut! Boyfriend! Girlfriend! Rock star! Jalapeño popper!)

Of course, I can't wear a black turtleneck and Levis every day—I'd look like a mime. It can be a bit harder for women to wear a self-styled uniform. Our staples aren't as standard, our trends change more quickly, and as we continue to work toward full equality in the workplace, showing up to a professional office in a hoodie is probably a pipe dream, even if we're the boss. But I still envied Zuckerberg. Not

> SINCE WE EACH HAVE A LIMITED AMOUNT OF MENTAL ENERGY FOR THE DAY, I DON'T WANT TO EXHAUST A TENTH OF MINE BEFORE I EVEN LEAVE THE HOUSE IN THE MORNING.

just his hoodie (sooooo comfy!), but the simplicity of his mornings. Could I find a uniform of my own? I decided to find out.

Uncluttering the Closet

At first it seemed there was nothing flattering, comfortable, and versatile enough to make it from one end of my week to the other without me ending up dressed verrrry inappropriately at either the pulpit or the playground. The versatility most of us need in our various roles throughout the week can seem to make keeping to a standard set of attire close to impossible and certainly impractical.

Still, the idea of a simplified wardrobe intrigued me for a number of reasons.

First, getting myself dressed has always been a challenge. I'm just *not* a morning person. When Daryl and I got married, every morning during those first weeks he asked me, "Are you mad? Are you mad at *me*?" I'd stare at him blankly, trying to process what he was asking. "I'm not *mad*," I'd say, finally. "I'm just not *awake*." He finally learned to leave me alone for twenty minutes or so until my brain switched on. (Ten years into our marriage and two kids later, this is still true.)

Secondly, I'm not the trendsetting type, and I always feel a little off my game trying to figure out accessories, styles, and an ever-changing body shape. More power to you if you're the kind of person who just loves shopping for new styles and trying out whatever crazy thing the fashion world is throwing at us. I admire and respect you, but I do not for a minute understand you. I mean, really, overalls are back? Midriff tops? *BIRKENSTOCKS?*

Third and finally, since we each have a limited amount of mental energy for the day, I don't want to exhaust a tenth of mine before I even leave the house in the morning. *What shirt should I wear? How about the aqua blouse? Should I wear a skirt or pants today? Is mixing blues a bad thing? Do these navy blue pants go with aqua, or should I change into my khaki skirt? Skirt it is. Darn it, my brown tights are in the wash. Have to go with the black skirt instead. Black skirt, gray tights, aqua top. I need a cardigan. Black? No, that's too much black. White? Yes, good. But this one's too long, so it looks weird. This gray one? Hm. Gray/black/aqua? Gray tights and gray cardigan? Is that too old-ladyish? Gold jewelry or silver? Are tall boots totally 2010, or do they really pull the outfit together? Darn it, I'm late. Again.*

Repeat, every morning. Add a preschooler, a toddler, and a shifting postpartum figure to the mix, and you have a recipe for decision fatigue with a smattering of self-hatred thrown in for good measure. Each and every morning.

But was it even feasible to have fewer clothing options without looking frumpy, out of touch, or unprofessional? Could it actually be possible to look good, be practical, and simplify my mornings at the same time?

A few years ago, fashion bloggers and magazines started talking about capsule collections. The idea was to take a few staple pieces, a few on-trend pieces, and a few accessories, and combine them in unique ways to both streamline and enliven a wardrobe. There were only two problems with this. First, these authors often advocated buying a lot of new clothes, for which I lacked both the money and the time. Not to mention that purchasing a new wardrobe went against the spirit of uncluttering God had placed on my soul. Secondly, these articles often recommended adding bizarro pieces no person in ministry could pull off, no matter *how* cool they were. Metallic spiked choker? Fur vest? Leather pants? *As if.*

Since I couldn't be Zuckerberg and a capsule collection wasn't the answer, I felt a little stuck. My closet grew ever more crowded as I filled it with Target clearance rack finds and Kohl's Cash specials, but many mornings I still felt like I had absolutely nothing to wear.

The wardrobe dilemma percolated in my mind for months upon months, until suddenly Ash Wednesday was upon me.

"What are you giving up for Lent?" asked a friend.

"Um . . . I don't know?" I responded. Not a good look for a pastor. Despite my chosen profession, Ash Wednesday somehow manages to sneak up on me almost every year. Plus, some of the standard things Christians give up for Lenten fasts don't work for me. I don't drink enough alcohol to make giving it up noticeable, and the year I gave up sugar it wreaked such havoc in our relationship that Daryl made me promise never to do it again . . .

ACTUAL TRANSCRIPT OF A CONVERSATION WE HAD ELEVEN YEARS AGO:

> Daryl: Why are we fighting? What are we even fighting about?
>
> Me: *I don't know.* I JUST NEED A BROWNIE.

So food—or at least my #1 vice food—was out. In previous years I'd given up television or listening to the radio in the car. I'd taken on spiritual practices like journaling or playing nightly worship songs on the piano. This year my soul needed something different. Something that could help shock me out of my routine and unclutter more space for God in my inner life.

Then it hit me. Maybe this Lent I could pare down my wardrobe, simplify my mornings, and eliminate my daily closet-initiated decision fatigue all at the same time. How? I would give up wearing colors.

My closet overflowed with color. Coral-peachy tops, brightly patterned dresses, checkered pants, teal sweaters. When Daryl and I were first dating I commented that he wore a ton of gray and brown.

"They're called neutrals," he told me. I asked him why anyone would wear neutrals when they could wear funs.

"That's not a thing," he said. Whatever.

Black, White, and Denim All Over

For my Lenten wardrobe discipline, I didn't want to pare down to just black. I'd look like I was in mourning, and I'd be constantly committing my husband's #2 fashion pet peeve: mismatching blacks. (His #1 fashion pet peeve is shorts so short a person's butt cheeks are visible. I'm with him on that one.) So I chose a couple of accent colors that would allow me to have enough to wear without

> MY SOUL NEEDED SOMETHING THAT COULD HELP SHOCK ME OUT OF MY ROUTINE AND UNCLUTTER MORE SPACE FOR GOD IN MY INNER LIFE.

going shopping for anything new. I began folding all my colorful shirts and pants and dresses and stowing them in a bin. After half an hour or so, all that remained on my shelves and hangers were shades and combinations of black, white, and denim. Perfect.

Unlike previous Lenten disciplines like The Great Sugar Disaster of 2008, this one energized me.

"I *love* this," I told my husband, five days in. "Everything goes with everything else, and I have *way* fewer decisions to make every morning. It is *fantastic*."

It worked for my work wardrobe: gray skirts with black sweaters, denim tops with black pants, and black-and-white blouses with gray blazers. It worked on Sundays: black or gray dresses. It worked at home: jeans or yoga pants, black tank tops or my husband's ancient Stavesacre band T-shirt, all topped with my favorite gray hoodie. (See, Zuckerberg? I can do it *too*.)

Getting dressed grew exponentially easier. No more wading through dozens of options. Now I had three colors to choose from, and naturally limited combinations.

I thought of the woman of Proverbs 31, clothed not in the latest Pantone hue, or the greatest Israelite trunk show jewelry, but in strength and dignity.

She wasn't stressed out by the future, but found joy when thinking of the days to come. In the New Testament, Peter reminds the women in the church that their beauty should come from within, not from their trendy clothing or stylish hair.[6] I remembered John the Baptist in his camel-hair tunic, a wild prophet who looked the part, and Jesus himself, who took no suitcase on his peripatetic preaching tour. The simplicity of my wardrobe brought me near-constant joy.

An Important Balance

It isn't that our appearances *don't* matter. Dressing appropriately for our vocations is important; I probably wouldn't last long at my church if I decided to preach barefoot, for example, or to get an inappropriate facial tattoo. (Are there *appropriate* facial tattoos? Probably not. Only Mike Tyson is Mike Tyson.) Going too far against social norms or looking like I didn't care about my appearance would hamper my ministry—not because our congregation is overly appearance-oriented, but because wearing things that clearly say "I don't care about my appearance" can be just as distancing as spending hours in front of the mirror each morning.

An uncluttered closet still needs to check all the boxes for meeting the needs of your profession. Living un-cluttered doesn't have to mean living in an uncaring way—in fact, it is just the opposite. Being mindful of our vocations—business, education, sales, ministry, parenthood, medicine—is an important key to uncluttering. There are times I need a polished, fitted, professional suit. Not often, but when I need it, I need it. It matters that it's pressed and clean. It matters that it isn't missing a button. It matters that my hem hits above my knee at the right spot. These things matter not because Jesus would love you or me less in tattered jeans and a hoodie, but because we want to be intentional about what our appearance communicates. It was true in the prophet Samuel's day and it is true today: people definitely look at the outward appearance, and the Lord looks at the heart,[7] but if our appearance is socially inappropriate or self-aggrandizing, our appearance can *affect* other people's hearts.

> LIVING UNCLUTTERED DOESN'T HAVE TO MEAN LIVING IN AN UNCARING WAY – IN FACT, IT IS JUST THE OPPOSITE.

Victoria Weinstein, blogger over at *Beauty Tips for Ministers* (tagline: "Because you're in the public eye and God knows you need to look good!") fights the frump that sometimes creeps into professional Christian circles when folks decide they're too spiritual to care about whether their pants fit properly or the fact that they last trimmed their toenails in 1963. Notes

Weinstein, "We are not souls whose bodies are afterthoughts. When we show up, we must communicate that we are clear about our personhood, our role, and the institutions and ideals we represent."[8] That's true whether we're in boardrooms or on the playgrounds.

Weeks into my black-denim-white Lenten experiment I realized I was still holding my breath, waiting for someone to say something. I was living, at least in part, for an invisible audience of my own. No one commented on it. No one even noticed. Turns out I think about what I'm wearing approximately 100 percent more than anyone else does. Wish someone had taught me that back in junior high.

After its forty days, Lent came to an end. I busted out a brightly flowered dress for Easter Sunday, singing with our beloved congregation about Jesus' resurrection from the dead while swathed in blues and yellows. The dress felt good. Easter-happy. Yet after worship I put it on a hanger and shoved it to the back of my closet.

"I think I'm going to keep the experiment going," I told Daryl.

"I think you should," he said.

It's been nearly a year, and now when I get dressed, I have time to clear my head, settle my thoughts, go over my calendar, talk to Jesus. I have time to look into the eyes of my kids (often while yelling, "DON'T TOUCH THE FLATIRON, IT'S HOT!"). I only make two or three decisions in my closet instead of a dozen or more.

A few months after Easter I dropped the bin of bright pink T-shirts and light blue pants and crazy patterned dresses off at Goodwill. I kept a couple of dresses—even I need a pop of color once a month or so—and a bin of maternity clothes—you never know!—but I haven't missed the rest one bit. Turns out Mark Zuckerberg was on to something. Not so much Facebook, but the uniform thing? Gotta give him credit for that.

New Stuff

STOP SHOP(PING) AND ROLL

Help me now, 'cause I never,
never need the one I want.

Teach me now, 'cause I never,
never want the one I need.

–Jake Armerding, "The Fleece"

Though I'm as close to a fashionista as I am to a golden retriever, I still buy plenty of clothes. Even today, after nearly a year of uncluttering, there are two shirts hanging in my closet with the tags still on. Sure, they're black and gray—part of my new wardrobe norm—but they've been there for months, and I have yet to wear them because—guess what?—I didn't actually need them.

Old habits? They die hard.

I'll admit that there's nothing quite like the rush of coming home with *just* the right gift for a friend, or a pair of on-trend shoes that make me feel like a million bucks. If clothes shopping isn't your temptation, odds are you shop for *something*. My glamorous sister (Caroline) is a danger to her wallet in Sephora. My deer-hunting sister (Caitlyn) can't be trusted with spare cash at Cabella's. My husband pooh-poohs the number of skirts I think I need, but the man has little self-control when it comes to Costco or the Apple store. Buying not only feels good; it can make us feel powerful, too. As my friend Chris once put it, "I get pleasure in the act of purchasing."

Yet this journey toward greater Christian simplicity had me asking: *Why* did I keep buying? After all the hard work of uncluttering closets and garage and drawers and car trunks (yes, even *they* were full, I'm embarrassed to admit), I fully agreed with Ann Patchett, who, in her essay "My Year of No Shopping," wrote, "What I really *needed* was less."[9] Uncluttering would only be a short-term solution to the too-muchness of it all if I continued to shop for things I didn't legitimately need.

Months into the experiment, I could already see our shelves beginning to fill again—Christmas presents for the kids, the latest cooking appliance fad, and hand-me-downs from dear folks at church were taking their toll. But the biggest offender wasn't the grandparents or the holiday madness or even those ubiquitous kids' meal toys; it was me. Me! *I* kept buying stuff. Turns out relying on self-control, or even the fact that I was about to publish a book telling *other people* how to unclutter *their* lives, wasn't enough. I needed to get to the bottom of why I shopped for nonessential things. Why do *any* of us?

The Dropping Shopping Experiment

"I've got it!" I crowed, my arms flung wide in the middle of our toy-strewn living room, announcing to Daryl I'd forever solved our shopping dilemma. "I'll stop shopping! We both will!" He looked up from the thick theology book in his hands—titled something nonsensical like *On Being* or *Why We Are*—and gave me a thumbs-up. Besides his affinity for buying food in bulk and the latest Apple gadgetry, Daryl is all about saving money. If I ever told him I'd decided not to wear deodorant ever again to save us $3.74 a month, he'd be tempted to give it a thumbs-up, too.

This was far from a revolutionary idea—minimalists and hipsters and Green Peace and my tinfoil reusing frugalista grandmother have recommended buying next to nothing for decades. Christians have long held that possessions can clutter not just the shelves but the spirit. One of the ancient Desert Mothers, Syncletica, once wrote, "We do not even want to possess what we need, because we fear God."[10] With the fear not only of God but of falling back into my old clutter-loving habits, I decided I wouldn't purchase a single nonessential thing for six months. Though the knowledge that I was in good company with both a *New York Times* columnist *and* every monk who'd ever lived was heartening, I nevertheless sped rapid-fire through the stages of grief.

Denial: I don't have a shopping problem!

Anger: This is a stupid idea!

Bargaining: What if I just buy things that are on sale? At Target? Under ten dollars?

Depression: This is the worrrrrst.

Acceptance: Alright, *fine.*

Beginning the experiment was easy. I stepped away from my habitual purchasing places—the big-box stores, the local boutique, the mall. When I was in doubt of what constituted a genuine need, I consulted with Daryl, whose definition of "genuine need" basically boils down to food, shelter, oxygen, and the occasional software upgrade. (Him: "Don't you already *have* a pair of heels?" Me: "Yes, sweetie. Most women have *several* of them.") My one area without limits was books—Daryl and I both mark up our books (which the library apparently frowns upon because "that's rude," or whatever)—so I could purchase those whenever I liked.

Since I'm not a *huge* shopper, I thought the elimination of hobby shopping wouldn't be very noticeable. I was wrong. After decades of occasionally but regularly purchasing things I liked, things that made me happy, things that looked cute or boosted my mood or filled that handbag-shaped hole in my heart, the struggle was real. My closet sufficient, my pantry stocked, my bookshelves bursting, there was nothing that I needed, yet my hunger was unabated. Why was I so bugged about not shopping when I didn't even enjoy it that much to begin with?

There's a great skit from *The Bob Newhart Show* where a woman comes in to visit a psychologist— played by Newhart—because she suffers from a deep fear that she will be buried alive in a box. He listens to her halfheartedly, and then tells her there's a revolutionary two-word treatment that can cure her. The woman lights up like a neon sign.

"Really?" she asks. She's been to no shortage of therapists, and no one has been able to cure her fears. She takes out a pen and paper and leans in.

He straightens up, looks her straight in the eyes, and says, firmly and loudly, "Stop it!"

She is, quite rightly, perplexed.

"Stop it?" she asks. "So...what are you saying?"

"Stop it," he says. "Stop it!" When she protests, telling him that she's *tried*, that obviously if she could stop being afraid she *would*, that there must be something underlying her fear since it's been with her since childhood, he sighs and concludes, "Stop it. Or *I'll* bury you alive in a box."[11]

A good doctor diagnoses the real issue, not merely the symptom. I'd been trying to stop shopping when shopping wasn't my disease. Rather than asking "What would Jesus buy?" or even "What do I truly need?" the question became, "*Why* am I shopping?" Turns out Jesus is a really good doctor, and a proper diagnosis was at hand.

Insatiable

I speak at MOPS (Mothers of Preschoolers) gatherings from time to time, and one thing that always seems to get a positive reaction from the room is talking about going to Target alone.

"Aahhhhh," the women exclaim, in unison. There's nothing like uninterrupted shopping time without kids in an affordable-but-still-very-chic clothing aisle. And there are such *deals*!

It feels good to find a bargain, to have an outing. Moms (and dads!) of preschoolers hunger for reminders that we are people, too, not just snack-dispensers, car-seat-bucklers, and butt-wipers. I understand the relief that comes in experiencing that we are still us, individuals with gifts and callings that include but are not

> MY CLOSET SUFFICIENT, MY PANTRY STOCKED, MY BOOKSHELVES BURSTING, THERE WAS NOTHING THAT I NEEDED, YET MY HUNGER WAS UNABATED.

limited to the holy monotony of caring for wee ones. I know firsthand the relief that comes in reconnecting who we were before our children and who we are apart from them. This consolation drives much of the real power of nabbing a well-fitting pair of jeans on the clearance rack for $15.97—pouncing on a good buy like that feels *great*. Home: a mess of toys. Dinner: not ready. Kids: poopy, peanut-butter smeared, and with Dad. Me: chic, stylish, and unburdened once again. At least for the moment.

Yet those jeans will go out of style, I will experience another frustrating day at the office, the kids will eventually miss their naps and turn into crank-a-saurs, and before I know it, I need another fix. It's easy to read our appetites as hunger for one thing when really, they may indicate a different type of hunger altogether. My hunger for a quick purchase, a rewarding trip to a big-box store, was masking a deeper, God-given hunger. A hunger for respite, for renewal, and for tangible results—all three a break from the mundane, everyday things of work and home. I needed a respite from the monotony, renewal for my worn-out soul, and tangible results that I'd accomplished something besides yet another load of laundry, pastoral call, wiped nose, or chicken dinner. In the everydayness, I craved newness and novelty. Don't we all?

Shopping met each of these desires. It's why so many of us head out to the store on a whim, when we have a moment to ourselves, or after that ten dollar birthday check from grandma shows up. (I'm in my mid-thirties. She's still sending them. Bless.) Shopping meets these needs, and the needs are real. In fact, the needs are *God-given*. But here's the thing: shopping doesn't *ultimately* satisfy them. It won't. It can't. A day, a week, a month later the same needs surface again, and the hunger still gnaws. Purchases wear out, shelves fill up, trends change. Shopping meets our deep hunger for intangible, eternal assur-

> MY HUNGER FOR A QUICK PURCHASE, A REWARDING TRIP TO A BIG-BOX STORE, WAS MASKING A DEEPER, GOD-GIVEN HUNGER.

ance that we are seen and valued and loved—with a temporal, *temporary* fix. We are starving, and our consumer-centric culture wants to feed us with cotton candy. God wants to feed us with steak. For free. Isaiah 55 puts it this way:

> Come, all you who are thirsty,
>   come to the waters;
> and you who have no money,
>   come, buy and eat!
> Come, buy wine and milk
>   without money and without cost.
> Why spend money on what is not bread,
>   and your labor on what does not satisfy?
> Listen, listen to me, and eat what is good,
>   and you will delight in the richest of fare.[12]

In a fast-food world, God offers us a priceless, satiating feast. In a parched culture, Jesus gives unending living water. While shopping is a treadmill of endless want and unmet desire—that couch is *so* last season! —God presents us with the truth of who he is and who we are. He is the one who satisfies. In him and through him and because of him: we are enough. In him and through him and because of him: we *have* enough.

It isn't that shopping is bad in and of itself. Shopping is largely neutral, and the desire for new things is written into our creaturely DNA. It's one of the reasons

God's promise in the book of Revelation that one day he will make "everything new"[13] is so profoundly alluring—this is what we *want*. Craving newness isn't wrong. It's when this desire begins to deter us from the deeper ends God designed us for—worship, community, fellowship, virtue—that it becomes a net negative on both our bank account and our soul. I'd begun identifying my true hunger, but I needed some help figuring out how to sate it.

> WHILE SHOPPING IS A TREADMILL OF ENDLESS WANT AND UNMET DESIRE, GOD PRESENTS US WITH THE TRUTH OF WHO HE IS AND WHO WE ARE.

Redeeming the Time

After battling alcohol addiction and getting sober, Anne Lamott wrote that she needed to discover what actually filled her up. "It was so strange. I was once again the world's oldest toddler. I walked around peering down as if to look inside my stomach, as if it was one of those front-loading washing machines."[14] Though my shopping probably didn't reach the level of an addiction—I hadn't drained our bank account; I rarely hobby shopped more than an hour or two each month—it still left a hole. If hobby shopping wasn't fully satisfying, *not* hobby shopping was less satisfying still. I needed satiation.

As always, I wanted it right now and all at once. As always, God worked more slowly. Pixy Stix can be ingested in a second; a fine meal needs to be savored. To begin finding God's cure, I began slowly taking small bites of more lasting pleasures. Exercise fills, so Daryl and I invested in a rowing machine. Friendships fill, so I dedicated one evening every couple of weeks as "girlfriend" night and went on walks with friends old and new. Music fills, so I began learning to sit at the piano or pick up the guitar rather than logging on to an online shopping site.

I want to go shopping, I'd pray. *Show me what you'd have me do instead. What would satisfy me more and longer?*

It wasn't easy. Instant gratification is, well, gratifying. Instantly. The slow growth of the soul and the deepening pleasures of relationship and worship and friendship are gratifying, too, but they take more time. They are more complicated because they involve more than just me and my credit card. They also never promise to solve all the world's ills, like the smell of new leather or a killer cocktail dress. Yet this is the essence of the call to live as strangers and sojourners in the world, passing through a land that is already-and-not-yet ushering in the kingdom of God—that we build relationships with one another, seeking God and good over stuff and self. Sometimes that will be disquieting and discomforting. Always it will be nothing short of divine.

I miss shopping for nonessentials. I do. A trip to the supermarket for milk and eggs is nowhere near as fun as a trip to the store for whatever on-trend top will make me feel cool again, if only for a moment. But the seeds of friendship, worship, service, music, and community grow ever more satisfying. Investing in the deeper things has deepened me, too; a truth no less beautiful for being a little bit painful, a whole lot hard.

These days when I am tempted to head out on an unnecessary shopping trip, I try to remember the wise words of C. S. Lewis from his classic *Mere Christianity*: "If we find ourselves with a desire that nothing in this world can satisfy, the most probable explanation is that we were made for another world."[15] My closets *and* my soul thank me. Maybe yours will, too.

Technology

ELECTRIC HANGOVER

And the crack in the teacup opens
A lane to the land of the dead.
–W. H. Auden, "As I Walked Out One Evening"

Digital technology is an incredible thing. Without a cell phone I couldn't call my husband to tell him I'd backed the car into another hedge (not that this has happened more than, oh, three times . . .), text him to grab gummy bears on the way home (those are a need, not just a want), or check out whether the apple seeds the toddler just ingested mean a trip to the emergency room. (Answer: no. But why in the name of all that is holy did he eat the entire apple core?)

Without the internet it would be much harder for me to Facebook-stalk people I attended college with who are now running for Congress (and thus prompting hours of soul-searching, because what have I even done with my life?!), and keep up on the latest memes so I can be conversant with the young 'uns in our church's college ministry. I wouldn't know which theologian is in a loud, public Twitter fight with which other theologian about what God is truly like. (It's obvious to me God's most prominent attribute is his long-suffering patience, since he puts up with so much baloney.)

For all the ways the digital era has ushered in easier access to information, greater connectedness, and an avalanche of funny videos, it's a very mixed blessing. We look at our phones instead of our friends; we enter time warps during late-night web surfing; we live for the addictive gratification of likes and followers. We've all seen zombie-eyed kids after hours on a tablet, antisocial teenagers more connected to digital games than their peers, and strung-out adults spending real money on ephemeral things.

> WE LOOK AT OUR PHONES INSTEAD OF OUR FRIENDS; WE ENTER TIME WARPS DURING LATE-NIGHT WEB SURFING; WE LIVE FOR THE ADDICTIVE GRATIFICATION OF LIKES AND FOLLOWERS.

How do we know what is helping and what is hurting us? Doubtless new technology has always caused fear and anxiety to those steeped in the status quo. Scottish philosopher Thomas Carlyle called the steam engine a "fire demon."[16] Journalist Ambrose Bierce called the telephone "an invention of the devil."[17] My grandfather calls the internet "just another way the government can take money out of my pocket." (Grandpa's a little paranoid.)

Yet there is a notable difference between a steam engine, a telephone, and a personal computer. Notes neuroscientist Susan Greenfield in her book *Mind Change*, "One of the big differences between the earlier technologies and the current digital counterparts is quantitative, the amount of time the screen monopolizes our active and exclusive attention in a way that the book, the cinema, the radio, and even the TV never have."[18] No longer is there a cap on how much entertainment we consume, a filter on how distracted we become. Now we can stream *The Great British Bake-Off* for seventeen years straight if we want. If we get tired of that, there are eighty-nine thousand other cooking shows we can enjoy and four hundred bazillion other programs after that. There is always a new app, a hot game, a text message awaiting a response. There is always more, so why would any of us settle for less?

Beyond the seemingly unending content we can consume, digital technology uncritically invades conventional scheduling bounds and personal space. Notes Greenfield:

> You wake. The first thing you do is check your smartphone (62 percent of us), and in all probability you'll be checking your phone within the first fifteen minutes of consciousness (79 percent of us). In 2013, 25 percent of U.S. smartphone users ages eighteen to forty-four could not recall a *single* occasion during which their smartphone was not within reach of them or in the same room.[19]

It's an epidemic, and one we willingly suffer from. And it gets even worse. A *TechCrunch* study from 2016 put our digital screen time at five hours a day. Five *hours*.[20] In the time between when this book is written and when you hold it in your hands, that number will likely be even higher. The mental and emotional clutter is real, the time we lose is devastating, but who knows how to stop it? I sure didn't.

A Soul-Searing Truth

How many minutes a day does your smartphone alone steal? If you're anything like me, too many. Waaaay too many. We don't give those moments away on purpose, of course. Our time is valuable; it's precious; it matters. Yet most days we realize that, by the time our heads hit the pillow, we've missed out on some of what Mary Oliver calls our "one wild and precious life"[21] because we've become constantly digitally distracted.

Prolific author Philip Yancey lamented recently:

> I used to love reading. I am writing this . . . in my office, surrounded by 5,000 books. To a large degree, they have formed my professional and spiritual life. My crisis consists in the fact that I am describing my past, not my present. . . . The Internet and social media have trained my brain to read a paragraph or two, and then start looking around.[22]

If Yancey, a prolific author born in 1948, a half-century before the dawn of the digital age, struggles to avoid the temptation of the sound-bite allure of the internet and opt for a book instead, how are any of us expected to do better?

When I hold my own mourning sessions about the ways I invite digital technology to disrupt my life, it's the moments stolen from my kids that hurt the most. Each time I am on my phone and look up only to notice one of the kids needing my attention, my heart sinks. Andy Crouch, author of *The Tech-Wise Family*, writes, "An awful lot of children born in 2007, turning ten years old as this book is published, have been competing with their parents' screens for attention their whole lives."[23] Their *whole lives*. Think about that. If you don't have kids of your own, perhaps you have nieces or nephews or roommates or significant others who have had to similarly compete for your eyeballs. Is the guilt setting in yet? Yeah, I feel you. Yet this isn't simply a case of man versus machine. The problem runs deeper than simply your willpower or mine.

Journalist Bianca Bosker interviewed former Google bigwig Tristan Harris for a November 2016 article on digital addiction in *The Atlantic Monthly*:

> While some blame our collective tech addiction on personal failings, like weak willpower, Harris points a finger at the software itself.... "You could say that it's my responsibility" to exert self-control when it comes to digital usage, he explains, "but that's not acknowledging that there's a thousand people on the other side of the screen whose job is to break down whatever responsibility I can maintain." In short, we've lost control of our relationship with technology because technology has become better at controlling us.

Concluded Bosker, "Technology is not, as so many engineers claim, a neutral tool; rather, it's capable of coaxing us to act in certain ways."[24]

I don't know about you, but the phrase "capable of coaxing us to act in certain ways" makes me suuuuu-per nervous. I don't want to salivate every time a bell rings. Yet—when my phone vibrates in my pocket? It's nearly impossible for me not to look at the screen, no matter what else I'm doing. I might be up to my elbows in peanut butter or diapers, seconds before the start of worship, about to get amorous with my husband, or driving down the freeway (YES, I KNOW THIS IS NOT LEGAL), and I will look at that phone. It's not just haunting, it's potentially disastrous.

Creatures of Habit, for Better or for Worse

Saint Augustine wrote at length about how sin brings out our animal natures. Sin brings us down to our most base instincts, reducing our behavior to that of unwitting animals rather than humans created in God's image. Sin dumbs down. God raises up. The trouble with our buzzing wrists, dinging pockets, and vibrating purses is that each of these bells and whistles pushes us to respond in uncritical, unthinking, automatic ways. We trade the ownership and agency of our souls for passive receptivity. John Calvin notes, "[People], using free will badly, have lost both themselves and their will."[25]

Then we'll feel guilt (shouldn't have ignored the preschooler again) or euphoria (yay, that post got sixty likes!) or frustration (WHY does our neighbor keep texting me about the trash cans?!) or relief (thank goodness the picnic is postponed—there's a storm coming). We'll feel *something*, all because a tiny device in our pocket buzzed or pinged or rang or flashed.

All day. Every day. Into the night.

No wonder the digital age, for all its convenience, has also become the age of anxiety. Being constantly connected gives us no real downtime; it isolates us; it addicts us; it eliminates much of the space and silence we need in order to care for our souls. Little by little, we have become alone together, digitally cluttered and interpersonally isolated. We spend time near one another but don't interact. We fill our evenings with activities that are enjoyed alone, or with people who aren't near enough to us to see our nonverbal cues, hear our voices, watch our body language.

Technology is changing our brains and our souls, and not for the better. You don't have to take my word for it, though. The late Steve Jobs, founder of Apple, creator of the device on which I'm typing this book, didn't have an iPad at home. The very thing he marketed as something everyone needed? His children weren't allowed one. Perhaps he knew something early on that I am only now beginning to wrap my mind around: that less really is more when it comes to digital technology. That an uncluttered mind will always be sharper than one suffering from an electric hangover.

The problem isn't limited to adults and teenagers, either. I recently met with our church's preschool director to hear about next year's curriculum. "Have you heard of Nature Deficit Disorder?" she asked. "Kids are constantly indoors and on screens, so we are going to dedicate next year to making sure they touch a leaf." As someone raised in the Northwoods of Wisconsin, the reality of this need makes my heart ache.

If technology is messing us up, stealing from our souls and our families, keeping even our pre-schoolers disconnected from reality, what do we do? Jettison it all? Live off the grid? Trash the smartphones, resign from Facebook, light candles at night so we can read our original 1860s-edition hardback books? Or is there a way to live in this world without subscribing to all the mental clutter that can go with it?

> BEING CONSTANTLY CONNECTED GIVES US NO REAL DOWNTIME; IT ISOLATES US; IT ADDICTS US; IT ELIMINATES MUCH OF THE SPACE AND SILENCE WE NEED IN ORDER TO CARE FOR OUR SOULS.

A Better Way

Few of us are called to step away from all technology. (Can I get an amen? I'm willing to bet I'm not the only one who doesn't really want to learn how to milk a cow.) I'm called to my church and my community, both of which are connected to the digital world. My son attends a school that communicates largely through email. If I didn't text, I'd have no earthly idea what my youngest sister was up to, because that girl just will not pick up her phone. Not to mention that if I didn't have a functioning GPS, I'd end up in Tijuana twice a week.

> AN UNCLUTTERED MIND WILL ALWAYS BE SHARPER THAN ONE SUFFERING FROM AN ELECTRIC HANGOVER.

So the question becomes: How do we use technology without allowing ourselves to be used by it in return? How do we practice thoughtful, nuanced decision-making in the face of Silicon Valley's best and brightest, many of whom dedicate their careers to making the digital landscape ever more alluring? How do we live into the uncluttered freedom offered to us in the gospel of Jesus? Philip Yancey notes, "Willpower alone is not enough. We need to construct … 'a fortress of habits.'"[26]

What might these habits look like? How can I wrench myself free from my digital leashes, save myself from the electronic abyss, protect myself from the hourly onslaught of pocket buzzes, pings, rings, and tweets? How can any of us? Is it even possible? It's a question I'd been pondering for years with no real answers, until one day I hit a breaking point. I was addicted to my phone, to being constantly connected, to the quick dopamine hits of likes and shares, to the distraction that is the digital universe.

I'd been studying Galatians, and Paul's words about freedom started to follow me around like an earnest toddler, wanting attention, always right at my heels. "It is for freedom that Christ has set us free," he writes. "Stand firm, then, and do not let yourselves be burdened again by a yoke of slavery."[27] Paul's words referred first and foremost to the bounds of legalism and the law that the church in Galatia struggled to let go of, but surely this applies to the bondage of the digital world, too. If Christ died to make us free, then we must not let *anything* make us its slave.

My digital addiction had to stop. But how? "Maybe," I thought, "I can create a fortress of habits. Maybe rules can save me. That's it! No phones at the dinner table. No screens after 9 p.m. No checking my email first thing in the morning." This worked beautifully. For about a day and a half.

It turns out that willpower with digital media is the same as any other type: hard to maintain. Habits are difficult to form and all too easy to break. When we rely only on our own strength, we will nearly always fail. Think about it: How many times have you tried to start a new diet, exercise more frequently, or make a New Year's resolution only to have your resolve disintegrate within days or weeks?

IT WAS THE ANCIENT GREEK POET ARCHILOCHUS WHO IS THOUGHT TO HAVE SAID, "WE DON'T RISE TO THE LEVEL OF OUR EXPECTATIONS, WE FALL TO THE LEVEL OF OUR TRAINING."

It was the ancient Greek poet Archilochus who is thought to have said, "We don't rise to the level of our expectations, we fall to the level of our training." Yet the best training can't compete with beautifully engineered digital devices and the thousands of code-writers, photographers, graphic designers, and marketers on the other side of a screen invested in getting us to click, click, click. Willpower and habits aren't the answer. That's the bad news. The good news is, there is an answer.

We *can* outsmart our smartphones. Technology might run our world, but it needn't rule our lives. But there's only one thing that worked for me: unloading the phone.

Unloading the Phone

I didn't get rid of a smartphone entirely—they can be genuinely helpful devices. (Though some people go back to flip phones or even landlines, and I applaud them!) For me that wasn't the solution. Instead I simply unloaded absolutely everything I could from my smartphone. My phone is now just a telephone, a texting device, a GPS, a camera, and a Bible.

My settings are changed and password protected (with a password I asked my husband to set and keep for me) so that I no longer have internet access. I unloaded all my games; I purged my publications. My phone no longer has Facebook or Instagram, mobile email, Snapchat, or Twitter.

It wasn't easy. But it's awesome.

Every app I deleted was hard. I mourned not having easy Facebook access. I stressed over losing Instagram. I had a borderline tantrum about giving up my digital crossword puzzles. (Yes, I *am* that nerdy.) I justified keeping it all. ("I use Instagram for the church's college ministry!" "How will I ever know what my sister's dog is up to without social media?!") Yet with every single app I deleted, my settledness grew. My presence in the real world strengthened.

The thing about a smartphone is, it's always easier to use it than to not. So I simply eliminated the number of things I could go to for instant gratification and distraction. Now there's nothing to check, unless someone's called me or I've gotten a text. Because I can only post to social media from my laptop, I am no longer constantly digitally distracted every minute of every day. In long lines, I can read my Bible or talk to my neighbor. At stoplights, I have time to pray or look out the window or talk to the kids in the backseat. While cooking dinner, I chat with my kids (or, more often, referee their cage matches, because—a moment of honesty here—creating soul space doesn't make your kids into perfectly behaved cherubs overnight...).

Late at night my phone isn't a temptation, because it no longer links me to the endless internet. I sleep better. I feel better. I miss none of it.

Yes, it's occasionally inconvenient. I now make quite a few more phone calls to check businesses' hours or restaurants' menus—things I used to do easily with a screen tap or two. And every so often I have to get the password back from my husband so I can reload a web browser for a few days because I'm traveling and genuinely need email.

But I can't reload the internet without getting the password from him (a necessary safeguard for me, since self-justification is real and I'd reload Facebook twice a day if the decision was left to my own strength). He's been a great partner in helping me digitally detox, and a few months after he saw the difference it made for me, he tossed me his phone so I could disable the internet browser and put in a password for him, too.

What we've found in the months since our phones have been unloaded is that it's now a bit of a pain to get online. This has been a wonderful thing. Instead of mindless surfing, we've discovered something radical. How to read (again). In lieu of responding to constant push notifications, we've begun to find more time to be hospitable with our neighbors.

It's not about giving up technology. It's about freeing our souls so we can wring the most out of this one life we're given. It's about entering into family and friend and neighborhood space unencumbered by having the entire human race buzzing about in our pockets. It's about fewer dings and pings and more talking and listening. It's about space and peace and rest and grace.

My electric hangover has subsided. No longer am I haunted by sleepless nights and headachy days. Instead, I've found a new way forward. Radical? Perhaps. Countercultural? Definitely. Uncluttered? To the max. And I wouldn't have it any other way.

Schedule

KNOWING NO

The difference between successful people and really successful people is that really successful people say no to almost everything.

–Warren Buffett

When I was eleven months pregnant with our second child (okay, okay, it was only eight-and-a-half, but it *felt* like eleven), I picked up our three-year-old at preschool only to have his teacher stop me at the door.

"You know," she said, reaching behind her for a clipboard, "Lincoln hasn't taken the bird home this semester."

I glanced down at the sign-up list. There was only one slot still open. His ten-day spring break. Also known as seven days longer than any of the other slots. Also known as a window of time that included my due date.

I hesitated. Just as I was grabbing the pen because that is what I do, I sign up for things, I say yes to things, I am a recovering people-pleaser and I will burn out in a blaze of glory before I will say *no* and disappoint *anyone*, the line of parents jostled me from behind and my unborn son kicked me in the lungs.

"Oof," I said, dropping the pen. "I'll get back to you."

That night at home I told Daryl we'd be taking the class bird home over spring break. He stared at me. Through me.

"That's *so* not happening," he said.

"But everyone is supposed to take the bird home, and we haven't signed up for it yet this semester!" I protested.

"We didn't make the preschool get a bird," he said. "Just tell them no."

As my guilt simmered all night like a fine pot of stock, I pondered this idea. Could I really just say no? Was it that simple? Not my circus, not my . . . bird?

Why say no, the saying goes, *when it feels so good to say yes?* Saying yes makes people happy—the boss, the spouse, the Sunday school director, the neighbor, the kids, the teacher, the friend. Saying yes is easier than saying no. Saying yes is *fun*. Yes to the late night, yes to the extra ice cream, yes to the additional project, the adrenaline, the speed, the stress, the sense that we will be infinitely capable and unencumbered by our own limits if we just keep saying *yes*. In the moment, saying yes feels *great*.

Yet we are finite. We have limited time, energy, and resources. Every *yes* we say is an implicit *no* to something else. *Yes* to extra ice cream every day might eventually be *no* to fitting into our pants.

> WITHOUT SOMETIMES SAYING *NO*, WE ARE NEVER REALLY FULLY SAYING *YES*.

Yes to the extra work project will be a *no* to date night with our spouse or dinner with our family or the long bike ride that our body and soul desperately need. We must treat our *yes* with care and purpose, lest we *yes* ourselves into the abyss. Without sometimes saying *no*, we are never really fully saying *yes*.

Yessing Ourselves to Death

Hi, I'm Courtney, and I'm a Yes-a-holic. Perhaps you're one, too. Yes-a-holics can be recognized by the way they walk (quickly), talk (with overtones of self-importance), and listen (not well). They're often spotted multitasking while in grocery lines, paying no attention in meetings, and staring blankly at their computer screens at 11 p.m. wondering how they will fit it all in. Anybody with me?

My default is *yes*. Yes, I'll take that on. Yes, I'll sign up for that. Yes, I can fit that into my schedule. I'll be right over. I'll write another sermon; I'll shop eternally for on-trend but completely appropriate shoes; I'll bring vegan, nut-free, gluten-free cupcakes. I'll do it all without breaking a visible sweat, though I'll be vibrating like a hummingbird with internal anxiety, because once again I've said too many *yeses* and there's no earthly way I can do all of the things I've agreed to do. Then I wonder why my soul is so exhausted I haven't spent more than five minutes with Jesus in two weeks and those were when I was *driving*. And I'm a *pastor*.

It has to stop, friends. In an increasingly connected age when we're expected to be available 24/7, to assimilate and parse more and more information, to cram activities and events and preschool birds into every nook and cranny of our lives, saying no is both radical and essential. It's also biblical. Take Daniel, for example. He said no to the rulers of Babylon when they commanded him to eat the king's rich food, consuming instead only vegetables and water. (Daniel and my juice-cleanse friends have some things in common.) Gideon said no to a sizeable army, trusting

God with his safety instead. Then there's Esther, saying no to remaining silent before a cutthroat king.

The greatest example we have of saying no is found in Jesus. God made flesh. The Savior of the world. Surely he was all things to all people and never said no, right? Wrong. Jesus practiced boundaries with love and strength like no one has before or since. He regularly said no to preaching, teaching, and healing anxious crowds so he could walk dusty paths up desert mountains to be alone with his Father. He said no to the benevolent mob who wanted to make him their king. Out of all Israel, he chose just twelve disciples with whom to share daily life. Out of those, he chose only three for his inner circle—Peter, James, and John.

> THE GREATEST EXAMPLE WE HAVE OF SAYING NO IS FOUND IN JESUS.

How was he able to keep such boundaries, to know which requests to accept and which to turn down? Jesus said no to thousands of people and requests and needs because he was clear on his mission. He knows who he is—God's beloved son. He knows why he came—to bring God's kingdom. He kept his mission ever before him.

This same Jesus invites us to understand who we are, whose we are, and what our mission is. For example, as pastors, Daryl and I have front-row seats to a steady stream of need in our community. From the grieving widow, to the lonely single mom, to the financially strapped college student, to the hungry homeless man, to the refugee seeking asylum, the list of struggles is long. In light of that, it can be tough to keep our family boundaries intact. Storytime with a toddler can quickly pale in comparison to speaking at a town meeting or organizing a much-needed relief program for a disaster area. How could we say no to the needs of so many in order to say yes to our two littles? Because God calls us to parenthood, too.

With our small children, we have realized that family dinners and reading to our boys before bed are the priority that makes the most difference to them. We agreed that we would strive to be together as a family for either dinner or bedtime stories six days a week. All four of us in the same room. It's a tall order, and it means some nights we eat dinner at 4:45 or 7:15. Often neighbors or congregants or friends or family members join us for dinner, crowding around our farmhouse table to pass the salad and get splashed by the toddler's mac 'n' cheese. But we make sure the four of us are together for that sacred dinner half hour or bedtime hour six days every week. There are exceptions, of course, but they are rare.

To say the nos that this family pattern requires, we have to keep the mission of parenthood ever before us. We are pastors and parents, and one can't come at the expense of the other. God entrusted these little people to our care, and we want them to know from their earliest days that we are there for them, not just for our congregation.

On a Mission

To what is God calling you? What is your mission? If we can learn to answer this question, we can begin to say no with greater ease, clarity, and peace. But if this seems an odd question, you're not alone. Companies have mission statements; people don't. Right?

Over a decade ago, when Daryl and I got engaged, the pastors who did our premarital counseling asked us what our marriage mission would be. "How will you be serving God better together than you could as singles?" Pastor Kevin asked. We looked at him blankly, with unblinking owl eyes. Serve God? Sure, we wanted to serve him, but we also loved each other and wanted to build a life together. And have sex and stuff.

Pastor Kevin sent us home with instructions to sit down and talk about whether God was calling us to marriage and, if so, how our marriage would honor God in ways our singleness couldn't. "Otherwise," he said, gently but firmly, "perhaps marriage is not for you at this time." Ballsy guy, Pastor Kevin.

As we pondered and prayed and I cried more than a little (because really, how *dare* he even *suggest* that we not get married!) we began to understand how saying yes to each other would mean saying no to other things. Daryl had applied to PhD programs in Scotland; I was looking to attend graduate school in the states. Someone would be saying no to a dream in order to say yes to a marriage. We needed to be clear about our mission.

Words like *hospitality* and *discipleship* began to spill out of our conversations. We envisioned our marriage as a haven for those in need of a place to stay, a warm meal, and a reminder that God loved them. We noted the ways we pushed one another in our faith. "Without you I'd struggle to tithe," Daryl admitted. "Your certainty about the love of God helps me trust him," I said. "Also, there are Sundays I'd definitely sleep in if I didn't know you were about to pull up outside my apartment and honk."

We came back to Pastor Kevin with a renewed sense of purpose, ready not only to say yes to each other, but to the mission God set before us as a couple. "Forsaking all others," as the wedding vows say, we prepared to say no to a whole host of things so we could fully say yes to one another, to marriage, and to God. I'm so grateful for pastors who pushed us to make it clear.

What is your mission? What vision has God given you for your vocation, your relationships, your household, your time? How can you keep that mission at the center of your decision-making and say no to all else that competes with it?

The Nuts and Bolts of No

Most of us will ponder and pray and get wise counsel about big things, like saying no to a job transition. But when the teacher asks us to take home the bird—a fairly manageable task, even for someone on the cusp of childbirth—how can we possibly say no? And if we *want* to say no, how do we actually *do* it? Often my lack of vocabulary for saying such a simple thing trips me up. I overexplain; I stumble over my words; I hem and haw and then circle back to the yes I shouldn't say. What are the mechanics involved in saying no?

There's a great short story by Herman Melville about a notary with a rotten boss who suddenly decides he's had enough. After years of drudgery, serving as a legal scribe without adequate compensation or respect, Bartleby is asked by his boss to examine a paper, and he hesitates.

Melville writes, "Bartleby, in a singularly mild, firm voice, replied, 'I would prefer not to.'"[28]

The boss is stunned. He asks again. Bartleby's answer is the same. The boss shouts his orders. Bartleby responds, quietly, with the same five words. After an entire career of responding to the whims of his bosses, the pressures of his office, and the needs of his clients, Bartleby decides to simply say no. It changes his life. It can change yours, too.

Like Bartleby, we can be polite about it. "No, thank you." "Not today." "I wish I could say yes to this, but my plate is full." When the ask is gentle, these kind responses can serve us well. But when the ask is filled with pressure, we must be firm. "No, that doesn't work for me." "I am not able to do that at this time." "Absolutely not."

Avoid giving reasons—reasons allow the person to whom you're saying no the power to decide whether your reasons are valid. You don't ever have to tell anyone the reason you're saying no. Sure, sometimes it's helpful ("I can't attend the bake sale because I'm having cancer surgery," is probably worth mentioning). But other times, giving reasons for your no cedes ownership of the situation to the person asking you for a yes. The only person to whom you need to justify yourself loves you unconditionally and died on the cross for you. To everyone else, a simple "I'm so sorry, I can't" is a full and completely appropriate sentence.

Saying a simple no or giving a general reason ("My calendar is full," "That doesn't work for us this week," "I'm afraid the date isn't available," etc.) is an important step in keeping an uncluttered schedule. There is part of your life that is accountable to no one but God, and saying a broad, simple no keeps that boundary intact. You need not explain your no. Even our closest family friends have learned that sometimes we will say no to things that are really important to them. We don't do it often, and when we do it might make them sad, but sometimes we need a Saturday night in as family so we can be fully present in worship on a Sunday morning. We say no so that later we can say a true, full-throated yes.

As a pastor, I'd be in an evening meeting six or seven days a week if I didn't say no regularly. So would Daryl. Our kids would be left to parent themselves, and our home would turn into Dirty Dish Lagoon™. So we attend the essentials—doing our best to keep evening meetings to three or four per week—and we say no to the rest. Much of the time I say no because I need time to prepare a sermon, visit a hospitalized parishioner, lead a college ministry event, or be a parent. But sometimes I say no because I legitimately need to watch a *Law & Order* marathon in my pajamas with a bucket of popcorn and a pamplemousse LaCroix. I'm that exhausted, that spent. And that's okay, too.

Start Small. Or Yell. Whatever Works.

My friend Paul is a retired engineer based in California who has done several big work projects in China. Over the years he fell in love with Chinese culture—the food, the people, the landscape. But he also had his share of frustrations. Because Chinese culture holds a high value in protecting a person's honor from public shame, his Chinese colleagues would regularly praise his proposals in their shared meetings and then send him letters detailing all the reasons those same proposals wouldn't work. This indirect communication added weeks and sometimes months to each project, and one day he had enough.

"I respect your culture," he said. "I'm working to understand it. But it would be so helpful if you could also keep in mind that in American culture, disagreeing in public meetings is totally okay. It's *encouraged*. You won't hurt my feelings. In fact, I would prefer if you let me know right away, in the meeting, if you have problems with a proposal I bring to the table, so we can solve the problems while we are here together."

There was a long pause. His Chinese colleagues stared at the papers in front of them, clearly uncomfortable. Paul worried he'd created a chasm in their relationship that might be irreparable. Then, one tiny woman stood up at the back of the room. She held up his proposal and pointed to it. The room held its breath.

"This proposal?" she asked quietly. Then her voice rose to a shout. "NOOOOOOO!"

"It was clear we needed some practice in saying a gentle no," Paul remembered with a chuckle, "but that was a helpful start."

If you, like me, are a Yes-a-holic, you too may need to break through with a shout. Even an awkward "no" is a place to begin. Don't let fear or politeness or societal expectations force you into a yes when no is the right answer. Easier said than done, I know— so sometimes, we may have to buy a little time when we are awash in the flood of internal pressure to just acquiesce to someone's request.

Brené Brown shares how she retrained herself to say no when she needed to, since it often felt so much easier to simply say yes. She purchased a spinner ring, and when someone asked her to do something, she required herself to spin it three times before answering them. As she spun it, she'd say to herself, "Choose discomfort over resentment.... Choose discomfort over resentment." Only then would she give an answer.[29]

A couple of weeks ago we had new friends over for dinner. When it was time for dessert, I noticed one of them picking the chocolate chips out of her pumpkin muffin and folding them into her napkin. Noticing my gaze, she looked up guiltily.

"I'm allergic to chocolate," she said. Talk about the dangers of being too polite to say no!

No is a full sentence, the saying goes. And perhaps if you, like me, struggle not to offer reasons or explanations or future promises in the moment, sometimes just pausing for a few seconds is enough.

A few weeks ago, some teenagers in football uniforms rang our doorbell selling magazine subscriptions. Dinner boiled over on the stove, and the toddler—unsupervised for 0.8 seconds while I answered the door—found a bottle of lotion and managed to wrestle the cap off. The house filled with the scent of lavender and burning rice.

"It would help our team so much," one of them said, handing me an order form and a pen. Daryl and I subscribe to exactly three things—one (weekly) newspaper and two magazines. We didn't need any more magazines. I didn't *want* any more magazines. Our budget couldn't *afford* any more magazines. Yet how could I say no to these two sweet high schoolers knocking on doors to help purchase new jerseys for their team? I hesitated, struggling to read through the list of options while the preschooler yelled from the other room,

"Mommmmm! Wilson's in *trouble*!"

"Can I take an order form and get it back to you?" I asked. They looked at each other and shifted from foot to foot. Suddenly I smelled a rat.

"Is there a way to contact you later, through the school, to place an order?" I asked.

"Uh, no," they said, backing down the walkway. "Never mind. We're good." Turns out the magazine sale was a scam, and those who gave those teenagers their credit card numbers later suffered from identity theft.

Sometimes a pause is all we need. Just a moment before jumping into an automatic yes. An "I'll call you back." A request to pray about it. A half second to call a spouse or a friend before committing. If the no is too hard or the situation too intense, pausing can be the start that we need. With even a few moments' critical distance, removed from the pressure of the situation, we tend to see more clearly. A pause can give us time to check our mission and remove the temptation to say a knee-jerk yes.

Beyond the practicality of it, there is often joy in the no. There's empowerment. Have you ever felt the weight of others' expectations fall from your shoulders when you took a stand, took a step back, took a breath, and said, "You know what? That won't work for me." It's *everything*.

Soul Growth Takes Time

Daryl once put a small potted plant—a red geranium—on a stool at the front of the church as he began a sermon.

"I want this flower to grow," he said. "And God can make it grow. God can do anything! So it shouldn't matter what I do to this plant." He took some big rocks and jammed them into the soil. "God can work around rocks," he said. Then he opened up an umbrella and placed it over the pot. "God can help this plant grow in the shade if he really wants to." Then came the pièce de résistance. He cracked open a can of Coke and poured it over the poor flower. A gardener in the pews gasped aloud.

"What?" asked Daryl. "God can do anything, right? Why should it matter that I'm creating such terrible conditions for this plant to grow?"

He used the visual example to illustrate that if we want our souls to flourish, we have to care for them. The growth belongs to God; the conditions—at least in part—are in our hands. A cluttered soul won't grow as well. A soul that says yes to everything will never get the chance to develop deep roots at all.

An uncluttered life is the opposite of a busy one. Certainly there are seasons where we will be busier— holidays, family visits, welcoming a new baby, caring for an aging relative, exams at school, or crunch time at work. My father-in-law is an accountant, and there is simply no way he *can't* be busy in the weeks leading up to April 15. It's his *job*. Busier seasons are part of the ebb and flow of life. The problem comes when we begin to be busy not just during short, isolated seasons, but all the time. When the adrenaline of rushing around like headless chickens becomes addictive, and we simply cannot stop. Then it's a red flag that there's something off in our priorities. That the conditions for the growth of our souls are imperiled at best.

A Necessity...or a Choice?

A Methodist pastor I know offers a blunt observation to people who tell her they're too busy. "Busyness is a choice," she says. "You can say no to it." The first time she said this to me, it stung. The second time, I felt angry. The third time, I sighed and realized she was right. If I am consistently busy all the time, it's because I have chosen busyness. If you are always busy, you have chosen the same.

It isn't even *enjoyable*, is it? Most of us don't love feeling that there isn't enough time in the day. At a certain point, we simply can't go any faster or push any harder. When I'm overscheduled and under-rested,

I find myself flinging the word at people who invite me to do things. "I can't go to dinner; it's a really *busy* week." Like suddenly it's *their* fault I've crammed so much into my life I can't sit with them over a table for a meal I need to eat anyway!

But wait a minute! You might be saying. *You don't know my life! I have bills to pay! I work five jobs! I have twelve kids! The kids are in baseball/gymnastics/water polo/aerial dance/pig Latin! We are remodeling the kitchen with hand-hewn barn wood from 1831 and my aging parents have three doctor's appointments a day but can't drive themselves!*

There are definitely things in each of our lives that are beyond our control and situations that land on our plates without any warning. But if we are consistently overbusy and overburdened, overscheduled all the time, we have made that choice. We have entered an age of frenetic, constant activity with increasingly less time to tend to ourselves, our families, our friends, and our souls. Digital connectedness amplifies this problem, as we cannot even escape to our homes at the day's end without the boss in our pockets or the social media crowds present in our bedrooms. The busyness train is always ready to leave the station. But do you know what? We can step off if we want to. It's a voluntary ride, and we don't have to take it. As Joshua Becker, author of *The More of Less*, notes,

"Busy is not inevitable."[30] Amen. Preach, brother.

I am, to be perfectly honest, totally terrible at stepping off the busyness train. Over the years I've gotten better at saying no—in part because I've begun to accept my limits—but stepping off the busyness train entirely? That's another story. Most pastors are in my boat. It is really, really hard not to fill up every moment, because there's a lot of need out there. How can I put my feet up and read a novel when there are thirty people in my congregation currently in the hospital, seven more who just lost their jobs, a handful of visitors who need a welcome call, a mission project about to launch, and a youth retreat that needs just one more chaperone, so could I...?

> IF WE ARE CONSISTENTLY OVERBUSY AND OVERBURDENED, OVERSCHEDULED ALL THE TIME, WE HAVE MADE THAT CHOICE.

If we are busy, the younger generations are being raised to be even busier still. A local high school principal recently told us that the biggest problem facing his school is not any of the usual suspects—drugs or violence or the breakdown of the family. The biggest struggle facing his students is that all of them are anxious and stressed out. Not some of them—*all* of them.

"Even *children* are busy now, scheduled down to the half-hour with classes and extracurricular activities," notes Tim Kreider in his article "The 'Busy' Trap."[31] Whatever happened to letting kids play in the dirt, poke stuff with a stick, and make cardboard box forts? I grew up taking piano lessons and figure skating classes, and there were weeks when even those two activities felt like too much, and they only filled up three hours a week. All I wanted to do was read Nancy Drew books, dig snow forts in the backyard, and irritate my sisters. (Come to think of it, that third activity is probably why Mom threw us into skating lessons in the first place...) I grew grateful for the presence of music and athletics in my life, but even one more scheduled hour would have overwhelmed me. The parents among us have to ask whether our ultimate goal is raising scholars, athletes, and musicians, or nurturing our children in the knowledge and love of Jesus and the care of their own souls. (More on that in chapter 12.)

> THE BUSYNESS TRAIN IS ALWAYS READY TO LEAVE THE STATION. BUT DO YOU KNOW WHAT? WE CAN STEP OFF IF WE WANT TO.

The church can be guilty of heaping endless activities on hapless parishioners, too. We plan initiatives, push committee work, and schedule countless meetings, often failing to ask: Is this what Jesus would have us do? Or are we neglecting the care of souls in favor of the running of programs? Are we courageously following Jesus, or are we simply unthinkingly doing *allthethings* we've always done?

Where has all this busyness come from? The pressure to fill every hour, to participate in countless activities, to work ourselves back into the dust from which we came? It certainly wasn't predicted by our forebears. In 1930, British economist John Maynard Keynes predicted a fifteen-hour workweek by 2030, when we'd all have time to enjoy "the hour and the day virtuously and well."[32] During the 1950s, a post-WWII boom in productivity, along with rising incomes and standards of living, led politicians to predict that by 1985, Americans would work twenty-two hours a week, six months a year, and retire before age thirty-eight.[33] While accepting the Republican Party's nomination for president in 1952, Dwight D. Eisenhower envisioned a world where "leisure... will be abundant, so that all can develop the life of the spirit, of reflection, of religion, of the arts, of the realization of the good things of the world."[34] How could they have been so wrong?

Busy Is…Normal?

Well, for one thing, life got more expensive. Costs went up, and wages didn't match them. Childcare is now more expensive than public college in the majority of states. Salaries have fallen while housing prices increased dramatically. But that's only part of the story. Our expectations went up, too. In an increasingly visual culture, we stopped being satisfied with ten-year-old cars and twenty-year-old kitchens. We feel pressure to keep up appearances and stay on-trend. This may be evident nowhere as much as it is in Orange County, California, where I live. Last year I drove by a three-year-old girl's birthday party at a local park. There were balloons and streamers. Awesome. There was a cake and candles. Great. There were three bouncy castles, a teenager in a Rapunzel costume and wig, and—I kid you not—a Shetland pony painted like a pink-and-white-unicorn with some sort of horn welded to its forehead. WHAT IN THE ACTUAL HECK? When I turned three, my parents cut peanut butter and jelly sandwiches into star shapes, and my five friends and I played at the local playground. They sang to me, I think. The whole thing cost fifteen dollars.

But at some point—driven by consumerist culture and media saturation and too much internet—we all decided that we *needed* more. More pretty things. More impressive things. More things, period. And someone has to pay for it all.

The rabbit hole goes deeper still. Even beyond the rising cost of living and our increased appetites for stuff, leisure scholar (yes, that's a real thing) Ben Hunnicutt writes, "Work has become central in our lives, answering the religious questions of 'Who are you?' and 'How do you find meaning and purpose in your life?'"[35] We consume more, so we work more. We work so we can consume more. And slowly, the working and consuming takes the place of worshiping God.

> AT SOME POINT – DRIVEN BY CONSUMERIST CULTURE AND MEDIA SATURATION AND TOO MUCH INTERNET – WE ALL DECIDED THAT WE *NEEDED* MORE.

Instead we worship possessions and experiences rather than the one who created us to find our true selves only in him. Romans 1 puts it this way: "Although they claimed to be wise, they became fools and exchanged the glory of the immortal God for images."[36] In Paul's day, this looked like idol worship—bowing down to statues made of metal or stone. Today, we still worship idols. But instead of bowing to statues, we bow to status, to self, and to stuff. We bow to busyness.

Yet God loves us too much to leave us in the busy trap. He created us to live lives free from the kind of hamster-wheel busyness that runs much of our culture and most of our world. We are called to work hard and faithfully and well—that concept is written on nearly every page of Scripture, too—but we are *not* called to sacrifice ourselves on the altar of productivity and activity. Instead, God asks us to let him order our days, to trust him with Sabbath, and to make space to hear from him anew. The work will remain unfinished, but because of Jesus, *we* will not. As Victor Hugo once wrote, "When you have laboriously completed your daily task, go to sleep in peace. God is awake."[37] We rest because he reigns.

> WE ARE CALLED TO WORK HARD AND FAITHFULLY AND WELL, BUT WE ARE *NOT* CALLED TO SACRIFICE OURSELVES ON THE ALTAR OF PRODUCTIVITY AND ACTIVITY.

No Looks Good on You

Bartleby wasn't the only one who knew the joy of saying no. I ran into my friend Megan a while back, and she told me her own story of the joy of saying no. Megan is one of the beautiful people. You know the type—effortlessly chic, constantly up on the trends, stylish without any apparent effort. Born with serious cheekbones. Born knowing how to *contour* her cheekbones.

When I ran into Megan in the preschool pickup line, she looked as gorgeous as ever, but something was different. I looked closer.

"You look really great," I told her. "Are you doing something new?" Maybe she was on a green smoothie kick like my neighbor. Nothing but kale and beet juice for seven days, and by day five arguing so loudly with her husband we had to turn on white noise to help our kids get to sleep.

"Well, I quit Facebook," she said with a shrug. "I have no idea what's going on anymore, but do you know what? I'm *way* happier."

That was it. Megan sported the breezy, unencumbered look of someone who was living her life without having to constantly chronicle and stage it for social media. She had said no, and now she had a settled peacefulness to her I hadn't witnessed before. All from saying one big, simple *no*. Megan's smile, her warmth, the lightness in her step, reminded me that I too had a choice. Lots of choices, actually. Modern life can be busy, chaotic, overwhelming, and nonstop. But it doesn't *have* to be. God calls us to something far, far better.

Called to a Slower Pace

In college I spent a semester studying abroad in Oxford. My first days there I walked around goggle-eyed at all the people whose brains were as big as the sky. Physicists, novelists, theologians. Translators of ancient languages, microbiologists, chemists, economists. Rumor had it that Thom York—of Radiohead fame—frequented the pub at the bottom of the hill, though I never saw him (and not for lack of trying). During student orientation, I hung on our program supervisor's every word as he explained how the lectures would work and gave us our library cards, house keys, and laundry tokens.

Then he paused. "This is a place for thinking," he said, finally. "Give yourself time and space to do that. If you're stuck with an intellectual conundrum or stumped by a problem or a paper, take a walk." He looked steadily around the room, making eye contact with each of us. "I want all of you to take lots of walks." Up until that moment, my academic career featured a lot of "try harder" and "pound out that paper" and "spend more time with language flash-cards." I used to plop my backside in a library chair and repeat, "Nose. Grindstone. Now." Take walks? That sounded...counterproductive.

Of course, he was the smart one; I was just a visiting student who chose to study abroad at Oxford because I never would have gotten in to Oxford. So I took his advice. And do you know what? My studies improved. When I took space and time and strolled the grounds of Magdalen College with its herd of deer, the aisles of Christ Church Cathedral with its operatic boys' choir, the steep hill up to our dormitory, and the cobbled streets of the town center, my ideas had time and space to percolate. My papers improved. My *thinking* improved. I daresay even my soul improved.

We *can* say no. Each of us can take a stand against a culture of more, more, more and faster, faster, faster, choosing peace and stillness instead and keeping a pace that is more attuned to the spirit of God in and around us. Whether our neighbors do or not, whether our colleagues or our friends or our family members do or not, we can choose to disembark the light-speed, high-rail, chrome-and-polish, runaway train of busyness.

Don't Even Buy a Ticket

Daryl and I quickly discovered we needed to be ruthless when it came to saying no. We blocked off hours on the calendar—family nights, date nights, downtime, and weekends "in"—months in advance, giving them a high priority. We blocked out time for soul care, for cooking and meal planning, for reading to our kids and to ourselves.

I ended up saying no to the bird. And do you know what? No one died. And had I said yes, the bird *might* have, since I was too preoccupied with my constant Braxton-Hicks and raging pregnancy heartburn to remember to feed myself, much less a pet-on-loan. We cannot do it all, and our lives will be shaped by what we choose to say yes to. So let's know *no*, using it wisely, willfully, and well. With each no we say, we draw closer to living a truly uncluttered life.

No is important. It's essential. It's amazing. But we don't say no just to say no. Slowly our nos began to uncover the profound truth that we say no in order to say one great, big, beautiful yes. What is that yes? Read on, friends. Read on.

Part II
THE GRACE OF MORE

The Secret of Simplicity

GOD FIRST

He has a solace in which he can rest more tranquilly than at the very summit of wealth or power, because he considers that his affairs are ordered by the Lord.
–John Calvin

Like many of you, the first thing I stumble toward in the morning is the coffee pot. If the toddler wakes crying, I pick him up, and he travels with me to the kitchen, the house still dark, my whole body leaning toward the earliest form of help and salvation I know. I bragged in graduate school that I didn't drink coffee, that caffeine was a crutch, that I'd never succumb to its bitter, brown allure, its promises of energy and bright-eyed early hours. I made it through graduate school, seminary, and half my first pastorate without so much as a cup. And then kids came along and I realized I knew *nothing* and I'd never actually been tired before. After running a marathon? Nope. Finals week? Not even close. Try not sleeping through the night for five-plus years. Now coffee comes first.

What comes first in your life? I joke about coffee, but anyone witnessing the liturgy of my day would quickly see that coffee is no laughing matter. Without it starting off the morning, I'm soon headachy. I stay bleary-eyed for hours. Grumpy doesn't begin to describe me. First, coffee.

But besides those first morning moments, what is first in my life? As a follower of Jesus, I am to put him first. Above all else. Over all things. Lord of my life. Of course, right? This is the basic principle of our faith, that we love the Lord with all we are and all we have—heart, soul, mind, strength. This might be obvious, but boy, do I struggle with it.

I became a Christian in my youth, and I've strived to live the principle of God-first ever since. Yet I find myself, over and over again, practicing not "God first," but "God and." God *and* stuff. God *and* busyness. God *and* smartphones. God *and* that cute new sweater from Gap. God *and* another side hustle so I could afford whatever fill-in-the-blank thing I decided I needed. God fought for attention and priority with a thousand other, far lesser things.

Scripture doesn't mince words on what those things are: it calls them *idols*.

Anything that comes before God in our lives, anything we place on par with him, anything that threatens our allegiance, bends our will, or weakens our love for God and neighbor threatens not just our space and our schedule but our very souls. You'd think that a couple of pastors (Daryl's in the same boat) wouldn't struggle so much with false gods, but I'll be the first to admit it. We do. We swim in the same water as everyone else, face the same temptations, have to work against the same cultural pull toward stuff and self. While Paul instructs us to "flee from idolatry,"[38] we dabble instead. When Peter speaks of idolatry as something "pagans choose to do,"[39] we entertain it a little. Why put God first when putting ourselves first is so deliciously tempting and so instantly gratifying?

> ANYTHING THAT COMES BEFORE GOD IN OUR LIVES THREATENS NOT JUST OUR SPACE AND OUR SCHEDULE BUT OUR VERY SOULS.

As Daryl and I practiced the principles of uncluttering, we began to realize that we couldn't make a thousand little decisions—what to take to Goodwill, how many events to put on the calendar, how to properly use our smartphones—without one overarching principle to guide them all. One great love to order all the others. *No* must flow from a larger, central *yes*. Yes to Jesus. God first. All the uncluttering in the world will ultimately be unfulfilling without this clear *yes*.

Not Glamorous, but Grace-Filled

Godly habits—like all habits—take time and effort to form. Do you know what the most-uttered phrase in our home was this year? What showed up most often in our spoken-word, greatest-hits of parenting? Not "Jesus loves you," or "I love you," or even "I'm sorry." Nope. What we said most often in 2017

> *NO* MUST FLOW FROM A LARGER, CENTRAL *YES*. YES TO JESUS. GOD FIRST.

within the four walls of our house were four completely unglamorous, borderline ridiculous words: "Sit on your bottom."

We had a five-year-old, you see, and we were trying to teach him table manners. So every single day, every single meal, we uttered this phrase nine or ten or thirty-seven times. He's a wiggler, this one. Lots of energy and little willpower to sit over a plate of asparagus and chicken for more than a minute or two. So Daryl and I, patiently and sometimes not so patiently, repeated ourselves like broken records. "Sit on your bottom. Sit on your bottom. For the sake of all that is good and holy, *sit on your ever-loving bottom*." That last phrase always made him giggle. It did not, however, entice him to sit on his bottom.

We repeated and repeated and repeated this phrase for a dozen reasons. Part of it was self-interest (I like a peaceful, civilized dinner table as much as the next person), but mostly we want Lincoln to be able to enter society as a well-mannered adult someday. To have a conversation over a high school cafeteria table and take a girl out to a nice restaurant for prom and learn the ancient art of table hospitality, which includes, but is not limited to, *not* buttering your hand before you hold someone else's for the prayer to bless the food. He's an incredibly smart and compassionate kid and a great listener 99 percent of the time, but for some reason the sight of plates and forks and cups turns him into a bolt of lightning. So we continue to work at it. And work at it. And work at it. Sit, sit, *sit* on your bottom.

Habits take time to take root. We may not be preschoolers anymore (though honestly I have days where all I really want is a carton of chocolate milk and a nap), but this basic truth remains the same. Sometimes the deepest, simplest, most important things take quite a bit of intentionality and care before they take root. Putting God first is like this.

Ordered by Love

My middle sister, Caitlyn, lives two hours north of Duluth, Minnesota. As my husband is fond of saying, "There's something *north* of Duluth?" (He grew up in Los Angeles. He can't help himself.) She and her husband and their four kids live beautiful, wild lives, raising chickens, canoeing down the river, showering with rainwater from a barrel in their backyard. You can't make this stuff up. Since moving north and getting interested in living more sustainably, Cait's taken up deer hunting. Deer populations often swell so big that some will starve if hunters don't pare down the herds, and between that and her goal of bagging a freezer's worth of meat for the winter, Cait's become quite the mighty hunter. Not to mention that a couple of hours alone in a deer stand seems like heaven to a mother of four.

Last winter, pregnant with her fourth baby, she realized her due date fell during hunting season.

"I'm going anyway," she told me. I'm a bossy first-born who can't help giving unsolicited advice, so I gave her some.

"Bring your cell phone," I said. The weather map of her area said it'd be ten degrees Fahrenheit. Ten. Degrees. Not to mention she'd be a hiking trail away from her car and a lengthy car ride away from any sort of medical professional.

"Oh," Cait said, stretching the word out to three syllables like Minnesotans do, "I won't need the phone. There's no cell coverage out there anyway."

"You're *nine months* pregnant," I said, as if she needed a reminder.

"I'm not waiting a whole year to go hunting, Court," she said. "This is my fourth baby; if I need to deliver it myself, I will."

What can I say? Girl loves to hunt. I'm more of a books-and-cookies kind of person myself, but I love this story. It shows the lengths to which a person will go when they really love something. You've probably not given birth in a tree stand—and neither has Cait, thanks be to God—but think of the borderline-insane things you've done out of love. I once sprinted across Harvard Square on a ninety-five-degree July day carrying a rapidly melting ice cream cake for my then-boyfriend, now-husband's birthday, because it's his *fave*. My parents took out a second mortgage to help put my sisters and I through college. My husband has actually let both of our kids barf *on him* when we came down with a raging stomach flu, because kids who are barfing need to know they're loved even—perhaps *especially*—then. (He's way holier than I am; I don't love *anyone* that much.)

When you really, truly love someone—or something— you find ways to put them first. The rest of your life falls underneath that top priority. No one had to convince me to make time for Daryl when we first started dating—I quite happily rearranged my work schedule, my school schedule, and my sleep schedule to spend as much time as possible staring into his green eyes. My grades showed a clear shift in my priorities, much to my dismay. No one had to talk Cait into going hunting in her third trimester, and despite my best attempts, no one could talk her out of it, either. No one has to tell my kids to finish their ice cream or my husband to watch UCLA basketball. No one needs to convince music fans that the Grammy Awards are a big deal, or food lovers to make time for the latest greatest restaurant in town. And absolutely no one has to convince God to make time for you or for me.

Yet I began my uncluttered experiment not by setting new goals and priorities but by trying to order my life around the words "can't" and "shouldn't" and "no" and "less." Now, no can be a helpful world, to be sure, and I definitely needed to learn how to say it. But it turns out you can't have a theology of *no*. Midway through my uncluttering journey, God wanted to teach me this *yes*. His yes. What would it look like to invite him—the one who made me, the one who *loves* me—to order my life? To set my priorities? What would happen if I put him first and let him sort out the rest?

Forming Habits That Help

One of the simplest and most habitual ways to begin putting God first is by attending weekly worship. Once a week, every week. As Kay ben-Avraham sagely notes, "We belong to a species that flourishes when we have regular body-motions to go through." As creatures of both body *and* soul, the routines and patterns we hold to can infuse us with the life-giving power of the Holy Spirit. Yet the habit of church-going is all too easy to fall out of if we don't keep that priority ever before us. I cannot tell you how many friends and colleagues Daryl and I met in seminary who slowly stopped attending weekly worship. Most of them were training to be pastors, but there were oh-so-many reasons not to go to church on a Sunday morning.

We understood these reasons, too: papers were due, kids were sick, internships were demanding. Those same voices echoed in our own hearts. "I'm giving the rest of my life to God," the rationale went, "so I get to keep my Sundays." This is why, early on in seminary, we committed to one another to make attending worship a high marital priority. We suspected that if we didn't team up, we'd stop going, too.

Still, I was pretty judgy toward all those seminary friends who'd faded out of regular worship. I mean, the tragic irony isn't difficult to see: How could we honestly coax our future flocks into coming to Sunday worship regularly if we sat *our* bottoms down at Bedside Baptist and the Church of the Holy (Down) Comforter?

This judgy attitude deepened until I woke up on a Palm Sunday morning with unusually severe cramps.

"I think I have to stay home," I told Daryl, rummaging around the medicine cabinet for the Excedrin. "I'm not totally sure, but I'm probably dying."

He looked at me and raised an eyebrow. "It's Palm Sunday, Court," he said, and reached into the closet for a dress shirt. I muttered some unkind words about how I should have married David instead because David was now a *doctor* who would *understand* I was in pain and not *guilt* me into going to church; downed a couple of pain pills; and limped out to the car for good measure.

"Does your leg hurt, too?" My Husband The Compassionate asked.

We attended a church forty-five minutes away, and it took me forty or so to start speaking to him again. Finally, I sighed. "I guess if Jesus can die on the cross for my sins, I can probably go to church with cramps." (Never underestimate the power of a little spousal guilt or friend accountability when it comes to getting to worship.)

Okay, okay, that's putting it strongly, I know. I'm not saying active crucifixion is the litmus test for who's allowed to stay home, and anything short of that means you need to suck it up and get in your pew where you belong.

In fact, "allowed" is precisely the wrong way to think about it. Commitments to weekly worship attendance are up to *each* of us to make. You decide what your values are—and, more importantly, why you hold them and what it is God is calling you toward or away from. For Daryl and me, the decision had already been made—unless we were suffering from something contagious, we went. Part of it was the freedom of a pre-made decision, but beyond that, we believe worship holds a claim upon us because of who God is; it's more real and true and lasting than our wavering desires, which can change with the seasons. We worship because God *is*. Whenever we can, we do that in the company of other believers.

Daryl wasn't pressuring me to go to church against my will; he was reminding me of my *deeper* desire, as I'd asked him to do. I wanted a life guided by the holy reality that God claims me as his own and calls me to the exhausting, euphoric, engaging work of being the people of God *with* the people of God, not my fluctuating feelings (those sometimes helpful but often untrustworthy guides whose direction changes from moment to moment, and who mostly wanted peanut butter cups and pajama pants and to not have to talk to all those people at church who were sometimes just so darned annoying because they didn't agree with me on *allthethings*). We both knew intuitively: only a steady compass needle is any real help in navigating the seas.

> WE WORSHIP BECAUSE GOD *IS*. WHENEVER WE CAN, WE DO THAT IN THE COMPANY OF OTHER BELIEVERS.

So on weeks where I wanted to sleep in, Daryl helped haul me out of bed. In seasons when his Hebrew homework threatened to drown him, I drove so he could study in the car. Part of uncluttered worship is leaving the decision already made in order to see what beauties emerge when you follow that deeper will.

In his book *Uncomfortable: The Awkward and Essential Challenge of Christian Community*, Brett McCracken writes:

Often we approach church worship from a posture of cynicism or apathy. Our heart just isn't in it. And for Millennials, for whom authenticity is a supreme value, nothing is worse than forcing yourself to "go through the motions." But if Christians only ever worshiped when their hearts were "in it" fully, worship would rarely happen. Sometimes "going through the motions" is precisely what we must do. The bodily motions of worship—singing, raising your hands, kneeling, closing your eyes—shape us significantly, even when we don't feel like they are.[40]

In other words, if sometimes worship is boring or rote or less than meaningful: you're doing it right. The everyday task of following Jesus will sometimes be just that: a task. There will, of course, be highs. Mountaintop experiences, spiritual ecstasies, that one particular song that sings through your veins like fire and freedom. But in between those fearless highs and the lows—those dark nights of the soul where the heavens seem shut up tight—there will simply be ordinary life.

> I WANTED A LIFE GUIDED BY THE HOLY REALITY THAT GOD CLAIMS ME AS HIS OWN AND CALLS ME TO THE EXHAUSTING, EUPHORIC, ENGAGING WORK OF BEING THE PEOPLE OF GOD *WITH* THE PEOPLE OF GOD.

As a Presbyterian pastor, I often wear stoles with colors that mirror those of the liturgical calendar. The color I wear most often isn't the white of Easter and Christmas (which represents purity and joy) or even the purple of Lent and Advent (which reminds us of both royalty and suffering), but the green of "Ordinary Time," making up the bulk of the church calendar. Most of our lives are composed of ordinary days—not highs or lows,

> IT'S WHAT WE DO IN THE ORDINARY TIMES THAT MATTERS MOST, BECAUSE THOSE ARE THE DAYS THAT SHAPE US MOST REGULARLY.

but simply worshiping the God who is the same on Easter Sunday as he is on any dragging Tuesday afternoon. It's what we do in the ordinary times that matters most, because those are the days that shape us most regularly.

I once heard a person complain to a pastor that she felt like coming to worship was just pouring water into a basket.

"Nothing stays with me," she said. "It feels pointless."

"Pour enough water in a basket," the pastor replied, "and the basket gets wet." Putting God first is a habit like any other. Stick to it, even when the feelings aren't there, even when it feels like pouring water into a basket, and it will change you.

A Faithful Pause

A brief interlude is necessary here. When it comes to weekly worship, Christians tend to fall into three basic groups. First, the Faithful Attenders who almost never miss a Sunday. Worship is woven into the fabric of their life as a primary thread. My own family of origin fell into this category. We'd show up not just Sunday mornings, but Wednesday nights and special missionary presentations and church family camp. As a teenager I once was so desperate to get a break from all the Jesus-centric festivities that I mixed together orange juice, bread crumbs, vinegar, and oatmeal in the kitchen, sloshed it into a bucket, and presented it to my mother.

"I can't go," I said. "I barfed."

"That's oatmeal and orange juice," she said. "Get in the car."

The second group is the Infrequent-to-Never Attenders. Folks who come a few times a year, or once a month, or not at all anymore. They range from personally very pious to barely committed to the faith, but their church attendance speaks of other central goals. Perhaps worship bores them or they don't want to give up an hour of their weekend. Some believe they shouldn't attend unless they *feel* like it, or that a church service wastes time that could be better spent helping those in need. Others say they'd attend church regularly if they could find one that "fit"—church as designer jeans rather than a community gathered to proclaim the truth and love of Jesus Christ.

As a pastor, these folks make my soul ache. Over time, the majority of the monthly attenders will fade into less frequent attendance. Many will eventually stop worshiping with a church altogether. Yet sometimes these seasons of space bring necessary grace that can't be received any other way. As Barbara Brown Taylor notes in her book *Leaving Church*, "If my time in the wilderness taught me anything, it is that faith in God has both a center and an edge and that each is necessary for the soul's health."[41] Leaving communal worship for a time and leaving Jesus are not synonymous. At times, a pause from the former may be what allows us to surrender more fully to the grace that is outside of and apart from and all around us: to the work of the Holy Spirit within. Later, as she begins considering going back to worship, Taylor comments, "We may be in for a long wait before the Holy Spirit shows us a new way to be the church together, but in the meantime there is nothing to prevent us from enjoying the breeze of those bright wings."[42]

And one final caution: perhaps the most dangerous thing about leaving church for a time is that in doing so we take our spiritual lives primarily into our own hands, to maintain them on our own. One of the best parts of communal worship is that it goes on regularly, repeatedly, no matter what state we may find ourselves in during a given week. Each and every Sunday Scripture will be read, the gospel will be preached, hymns will be sung, prayers will be offered. It doesn't depend on us to keep it going. As Jim Gaffigan said of his Catholic tradition, "If you haven't been to a Catholic Mass, don't worry, it's *still going on ...*"[43]

Yet beyond the Faithful Attenders and the Infrequent-to-Never crowd is a third group, and one that all too often goes overlooked. This third group is comprised of Christians who love Jesus but simply *cannot* attend communal worship for a season. Their absence is not arrogance or laziness; it is necessity. Perhaps they struggle with doubt and discover that their particular congregation doesn't welcome difficult questions or open uncertainties. Some have been abused by someone within the church. Others have witnessed a congregational meltdown because of a scandal or, worse yet, watched institutional powers cover up misconduct that needed to be brought out into the open to be made right. Still others work Sundays because their profession or financial survival requires it.

If you are in this third group, friend, know that Jesus adores you and will walk this road alongside you.

Let him nurture and heal you. Read works that fill you back up—T. S. Eliot's "Ash Wednesday" poems, Anne Lamott's reverently irreverent essays, and Martin Luther King Jr.'s sermons have brought church to me during my own desert seasons—and let the Spirit minister balm to your soul. Your salvation does not depend on your butt being in a pew on a Sunday. (Did you hear that? No guilt.) You are safest in the arms of the one who created and adores you.

A God-Given Yes

Scripture bears witness to the types of things God puts first. God says yes to people. To reconciliation. To joy. God says yes to coaxing us from our comfort zones to follow him anew. God says yes to courage, to listening, to hospitality, to good news. Sometimes God says yes to service; other times he says yes to rest. And sometimes God says yes to suffering. To loss. To grief. To dark nights of the soul. I wasn't so sure I was on board with that last bit. But I knew my control was an illusion, and I needed to release myself—space, schedule, and soul—into the hands of the God who created me.

> I KNEW MY CONTROL WAS AN ILLUSION, AND I NEEDED TO RELEASE MYSELF—SPACE, SCHEDULE, AND SOUL—INTO THE HANDS OF THE GOD WHO CREATED ME.

It was a little scary. When we invite God to order our lives according to his will and his word—the ultimate uncluttering adventure—there will inevitably be times when he will order our lives differently than we would have chosen. As C. S. Lewis paraphrases George MacDonald in his classic *Mere Christianity*:

> Imagine yourself as a living house. God comes in to rebuild that house. At first, perhaps, you can understand what He is doing. He is getting the drains right and stopping the leaks in the roof and so on; you knew that those jobs needed doing and so you are not surprised. But presently He starts knocking the house about in a way that hurts abominably and does not seem to make any sense. What on earth is He up to? The explanation is that He is building quite a different house from the one you thought of—throwing out a new wing here, putting on an extra floor there, running up towers, making courtyards. You thought you were being made into a decent little cottage: but He is building a palace. He intends to come and live in it Himself.[44]

We long for order and tidiness—and indeed, these are God-given desires—but the Holy Spirit also comes like a rushing wind and a blazing fire and sometimes what's best for us is a white-hot crucible or a great big mess.

And—praise Jesus—when we invite him in to order and unclutter our lives, he never fails to have our best interest at heart. What's more—he has the best interest of our neighbors and our church and our community and our world in mind, too. I was uncluttering my life for me and my family and my own soul, making changes because I'd arrived, panicking and afraid, at my mental and physical end with all the stress, but all the while God had something far bigger and more beautiful in mind. He wanted to remake me, as a small, simple step in remaking the whole world.

This might sound a little overblown, but the truth is that God works in the miniscule things to bring glory in the majors. As Eugene Peterson notes, "When it comes to doing something about what is wrong in the world, Jesus is best known for his fondness for the minute, the invisible, the quiet, the slow—yeast, salt, seeds, light. And manure."[45] As someone who spends a lot of time dealing with diapers these days, these words are of immense comfort. Small acts of obedience, glamorous or not, have eternal ramifications and everlasting consequences. There is great relief in this, for the problems of the world can threaten to overwhelm.

> HE WANTED TO REMAKE ME, AS A SMALL, SIMPLE STEP IN REMAKING THE WHOLE WORLD.

Yet God invites us to allow him to order our days, and when we are faithful with what's right in front of us, good will come. Sometimes we will be asked to do big things—and in those moments we must not shrink back from them—but most often we will be asked to do small, faithful things repeatedly. This is where the work of preparing soil and hearts truly begins.

Luke's parable of the mustard seed speaks of these small acts of ordering: "[The kingdom of heaven] is like a mustard seed, which a man took and planted in his garden. It grew and became a tree, and the birds perched in its branches."[46] It is telling that, in contrast to Matthew's description of this parable, which talks about moving mountains, Luke's talks about the growth of a single tree. The seed becomes a tree where birds find a home. And in that moment, it is enough. Sometimes we try to move the mountains when what God really wants us to do is be faithful in growing where we're planted so the birds have a place to roost. God's way of doing things is rarely big or fast or flashy. It's a baby in a manger, strangers gathered around a dinner table, a wooden cross.

The Antidote to Worry

When we put God first, giving him control, we don't give him anything he doesn't already have. But it is in giving up to God what is always and already his that we begin to be transformed. It's Abraham and Isaac all over again. Could God have taken Isaac without Abraham's consent? Absolutely. Yet it was in the releasing that Abraham was forever changed. And he received Isaac back—whole and unharmed—and with him, trust.

So how, then, do we invite God to order our lives with his yes? In the Sermon on the Mount, Jesus preaches to a crowd worried about their very survival—will there be enough food to eat? (Not an insignificant worry in a desert landscape prone to famines!) Will there be enough to drink? (Again, not a small worry in the desert!) Beyond that, will there be enough resources to clothe them? (This question is both one of resource and one of dignity.) Jesus says,

> Therefore I tell you, do not worry about your life, what you will eat or drink; or about your body, what you will wear. Is not life more than food, and the body more than clothes? Look at the birds of the air; they do not sow or reap or store away in barns, and yet your heavenly Father feeds them. Are you not much more valuable than they?[47]

Worrying is tied to a mind-set of scarcity, but also to one of realism. In Jesus' day, there often wasn't enough. Without refrigeration, food didn't keep. Without a social safety net, a broken ankle could mean starvation. Getting water from the well was daily drudgery, and when the well ran dry? Watch out. We face scarcity today too, no doubt, but in Jesus' day life on the edge was obvious, everywhere, and inescapable.

Still, Jesus instructs the crowd not to orient their lives around these things. Even though food and water and clothing were essential, there was one thing that was more essential still. He continues:

> So do not worry, saying, "What shall we eat?" or "What shall we drink?" or "What shall we wear?" For the pagans run after all these things, and your heavenly Father knows that you need them. But seek first his kingdom and his righteousness, and all these things will be given to you as well.[48]

Our heavenly Father *knows* we need food and water, clothing and shelter, love and friendship, purpose and meaning. It doesn't surprise him when our stomachs grumble for dinner or our throats get parched on a hike or we wear out our last pair of good jeans. The tiny, beautiful, mundane details of our lives are never lost on the God of the universe. The trouble comes when we go after these things *first*, clutching at and clinging to *things*. A closed fist can accept no gift. When we say yes first to the kingdom, God orders the rest.

The Hard Work of Trust

It's one thing to write about putting God first. It's another to live it. A short time ago, even as I began to realize anew that I needed a spiritual overhaul, Daryl and I found ourselves in a really tight spot. Rent had increased dramatically (an insane nearly 20 percent) since we'd moved to southern California, and we were slowly but surely being priced out of our condo. Moving to a smaller place wasn't really an option—housing a family of four in one bedroom would have been quite the squeeze, not to mention in violation of our county's housing codes—but buying something was out of reach entirely. Ministry at our church was booming, and I was already adjunct teaching at a local Christian college on top of that, so shoehorning in another part-time job wasn't an option. We were already quite frugal—I cut my own hair (sometimes you could tell), we only bought groceries on sale, and date nights were walks on the beach or popcorn on the sofa. We'd spent a couple of years vibrating with financial stress, arguing over whether we could afford to turn the air conditioner on when it was ninety degrees outside (I promised I'd sell a kidney if need be, but when the chocolate chips in the cabinet began to melt, I did too . . .), and praying. Boy, did we pray.

God, I begged one night, my eyes overflowing, my face pressed into the bedroom carpet, *You have to do something. We are at the end of our resources and the end of our rope.* Anne Lamott writes that her two most often-used prayers are "Help me, help me, help me," and "Thank you, thank you, thank you."[49] I longed to pray "Thank you," but for months, "Help me" was all I could muster.

Since there was nothing more we could do, we left it in God's hands. Amazing how often it takes total desperation before we do that, isn't it? Daryl and I began telling each other regularly, "God's going to do something." We didn't know what the *something* was—it could be anything from calling us to a more affordable area to having us house-sit long term for someone in our congregation to a straight up loaves-and-fishes miracle. God was going to have to move the mountain somehow. We strove to be faithful with our mustard seeds in the meantime.

> I LONGED TO PRAY "THANK YOU," BUT FOR MONTHS, "HELP ME" WAS ALL I COULD MUSTER.

There was no immediate miracle. There rarely ever is. The ache of worry still gnawed, the sleepless nights still plagued, the drumbeat of fear hammered away. But with the release of the reins, God gave us moments of unexpected, illogical, nonsensical, abiding peace. The kind of peace I might even call divine—not something we could summon on our own, no matter how hard we tried. Not something dependent upon our circumstances, for those remained unchanged. So we drank in this peace. We hoped. And still, we waited.

At moments the peace would evaporate, and we would wonder if our waiting was pure insanity. What were we even waiting for, exactly? Skywriting? A headhunter? A crash in the housing market? We didn't know. We were waiting for God to move, and trusting he had a plan. Reading to our toddler one night, I picked up a Mo Willems classic called *Don't Let the Pigeon Drive the Bus.* It's about a little stick-figure pigeon who thinks he has the chops to navigate a giant vehicle through the city streets. Needless to say, he's *not* a good driver. Midway through, I got the giggles and couldn't stop.

"You okay?" Daryl called from the hallway.

"Yep," I said. "It's just that, with our housing crisis, trusting God feels like letting the pigeon drive the bus."

A few nights later at small group, our friend Bill commented, "There's a particular joy borne of desperation, too, isn't there? When you have nothing left, God is there at the bottom." Time and time again, God was. Though there were definitely moments when I grew tired of letting the pigeon drive.

"Why isn't this easier?" I complained to Daryl one night.

"I don't think easy is what God majors in," he said. He was right, of course, even though I really didn't want him to be. One of the pernicious myths of the Christian life is that it will be easy. That idea is found exactly *nowhere* in Scripture. "Pick up your cross!" says Jesus.[50] "You are blessed when you suffer!" Peter reminds us.[51] Yet the myth persists. If the goal is coziness or luxury or serenity, the Christian faith is not where it's at.

Then, one day, much later than we would have preferred and with more than a little last minute breath-holding and hair-graying on our parts, we moved into a house—our very first, very own house—with help from a whole village of generous people. I'm talking George Bailey in *It's a Wonderful Life*-level stuff. Daryl and I stood at the window of our bedroom that first night, amidst stacks of boxes and piles of books, and wept. God hadn't given us a house because we'd been faithful; God had provided for us because *he* was faithful. The past years of stress and strain and fear had done their work, driving us to our knees, driving us closer to him. And where Jesus is, there is hope. Peace that transcends the events of our lives.

We prayed over each room, dedicating the house to the one who gave it to us. From the start we told our boys that it was God's house (something that brought confusion to our five-year-old, who kept saying, "But I thought *church* was God's house!"). Our dining room table was his. The guest bedroom and the kids' bedroom and our master bedroom belonged to him. The backyard and front, the garage and the attic. Each nail, every shingle, all the wires and tiles and pipes.

> GOD HADN'T GIVEN US A HOUSE BECAUSE WE'D BEEN FAITHFUL; GOD HAD PROVIDED FOR US BECAUSE *HE* WAS FAITHFUL.

"Maybe this one will stick," Daryl said, unpacking a few remaining boxes with me on a Saturday afternoon.

"Which one?" I asked.

"The lesson that God's way is best and we should leave him in charge."

"God first. Amen to that."

We continue to learn what it looks like to put God first, to accept both painful lessons and gracious blessings from his hand, ordering our lives with his love. But with our financial crisis resolved, God invited us to explore a new horizon, putting him first not just when it came to trust but when it came to schedule.

"I think we need to double down on keeping the Sabbath," I said.

Therein lay our greatest adventure yet.

Sabbath

RECEIVING THE GIFT

After mist has wrapped us again
in fine wool, may the taste of salt
recall to us the great depths about us.
–Denise Levertov, "The Depths"

There's an old joke I've heard that goes something like this: A man wakes up to the sound of rushing water and realizes that his home is flooding. He looks out the window only to discover that the whole *neighborhood* is flooding. In a panic, he does the only thing he can think to do: he climbs onto his roof to avoid the deadly, swirling waters.

This man isn't particularly religious, but if there has ever been a time to pray, this is it. So he prays: *God, please save me from this flood.* He feels a burst of comfort in his soul and reads this as an assurance that God will save him. A few moments later, a canoe appears. It's his neighbor.

"Hey there!" the neighbor shouts, maneuvering close to the roof. "Can I give you a lift?"

"No thanks," says the man. "God will save me." The neighbor shrugs and paddles away.

The waters continue to rise. Thirty minutes later, a speedboat comes motoring down the street picking up stranded people from trees and rooftops.

"Need a lift?" asks the driver.

"Nope," the man replies with cheer, "God will save me!" A few minutes later the waters begin to lap at the edges of the roof. Suddenly a Coast Guard helicopter circles overhead.

"Do you require assistance?" a rescue swimmer shouts down through a bullhorn.

"No!" shouts the man. "God will save me!" Then the waters rise above the roof and the man drowns.

When he arrives at the pearly gates of heaven (this part is terrible theology, but stay with me for the sake of the joke) and meets God face-to-face, he stomps his foot and shakes his fist.

"I'm not supposed to be dead, God!" he protests.

"You said you'd save me!"

God says, "I sent you a canoe, a speedboat, and a Coast Guard helicopter! How do you think *I* feel?" (Ba dum, *ching*!) Sometimes we miss the rescue that's right in front of us.

We are all in danger of drowning. I am. You are. Your best friend is, your neighbor, and your pastor. The person who takes your order at Chipotle and Beyoncé and your dad and the president of the United States and Big Bird. Okay, maybe not Big Bird, since he's fictional and all, but the rest of us? We need a rescue from the swirling waters of busyness and stress and work and producing and running and being constantly on the go. We need a rescue from the constant connectedness of the digital world and the obscene amount of on-call availability that cell phones have made seem normal. We need a rescue from our stress. We need a rescue from ourselves. The waters of too-much-ness lap at our rooftops; they threaten our safety; they overwhelm any ability we may have had to save ourselves.

> WE NEED A RESCUE FROM OUR STRESS. WE NEED A RESCUE FROM OURSELVES.

Yet perhaps we, like the man on the roof, are waiting for a rescue we recognize. A miracle. A burst of energy. Extra endurance to keep on keeping on. For years I prayed for the spiritual hardiness to be able to do everything in front of me, all the time, without stopping. To finally finish everything on my "to do" list once and for all. I quoted Isaiah 40 about how those who wait on the Lord will "renew their strength" and rise up with "wings like eagles" and all of that heroic stuff.

"Renew my strength, God!" I demanded. "I'm tired! Where are you?"

But God never answered my prayer for the ability to keep going fast and forever without ever stopping to rest. He never does. I'm convinced he never will. I wanted supernatural strength to carry me seven days a week, nineteen-ish hours a day, but God's rescue for his people is far more ordinary than that, and far more holy. He does grant us strength, of course, but not the strength to become perpetual motion machines. God has no interest in helping us become Energizer bunnies, but he has a deep longing for us to enter into the ancient and holy rhythm of work and play and rest. For the

GOD HAS NO INTEREST IN HELPING US BECOME ENERGIZER BUNNIES, BUT HE HAS A DEEP LONGING FOR US TO ENTER INTO THE ANCIENT AND HOLY RHYTHM OF WORK AND PLAY AND REST.

rescue of our sin-sick, overscheduled, self-reliant souls, God sends Sabbath.

The Gift No One Wants

Sabbath is a promise-rich gift—the command to stop once a week, every week, in the midst of the rushing water flooding our lives, to climb aboard God's peaceful boat where we will find rest. Sabbath-keeping is holding one day a week open to God with no work obligations, on-call responsibilities, or home front "to do" lists to be found. It is a special, holy, sacred, ordinary, recurring day, set aside (as Eugene Peterson puts it) for praying and playing.[52] In a culture driven by *doing*, and *going*, and *producing*, and *consuming*, it doesn't get much more radical than Sabbath.

It's no joke how overworked, overscheduled, and overcommitted most of us are—I'm guessing you feel that truth deep in your own soul, too. We've talked about digital distractions and drowning in clutter. Yet the need for Sabbath goes deeper than each of these things. The need for Sabbath is a profoundly human one, a present given to us at the start of creation, an essential—I'd even say *the* essential—tool for a healthy soul. Sabbath-keeping is *life*, and we need it now more than ever. To a culture that worships productivity, Sabbath is God's way of saying: stop. To a people that defines ourselves by our speed, Sabbath is God's way of saying: rest. To a church that all too often forgets its main mission of worshiping the living God, Sabbath is his way of saying: remember who you are. Remember *whose* you are.

Sabbath is radical. Stopping production, ceasing our striving, refusing—for one day each week—to produce, clock in, or keep track, is distinctly countercultural. It's borderline bizarre. This is how God works, though. He saves us by dying. Gains power by serving. Tells us that the greatest among us must be like the least, the last will be first, and we must become like little children. Odd as the Sabbath might seem, it fits right in with how God works throughout Scripture. But that doesn't make it easy. The great Old Testament scholar Walter Brueggemann calls Sabbath "the most urgent and the most difficult of all the commandments."[53] Let's face it: most of us are *doers*. If we stop doing—and not just for an annual vacation or because of an illness but for an entire day *every single week*, who will we be? Who might we become?

My youngest sister Caroline worked briefly for a decluttering company in the Twin Cities, helping elderly adults downsize so they could transition into condos or assisted-living facilities. One of the lessons her boss taught her early on was how to stage closets and shelves to cultivate a beautiful space. "You have to leave room," she said.

"If you smash everything together, it'll *always* look cluttered," Caroline told me later, helping me make sense of my overburdened bookshelves. "It's important to create space between items, and especially between groups of items, or everything visually runs together and it becomes a mess." What is true of our shelves is true of our days. Without a proper rhythm of work and worship, striving and rest, our days blend together into a cluttered whole. Sabbath gives rhythm to our lives, creating space between work and more work, a pause for the renewal of our spirits. Work is *good*; it's the rhythm of never-ending, unceasing work that will kill us if we let it. Too much of a good thing is no longer good.

> AS ALL OF GOD'S COMMANDS, THE COMMAND FOR SABBATH REST IS ULTIMATELY FOR OUR GOOD.

Beyond this, Sabbath is commanded by God. If we are following Jesus, we really cannot set one of the Ten Commandments aside for convenience or because we feel we know better. As 1 John puts it, "For this is the love of God, that we keep his commandments. And his commandments are not burdensome."[54] Notice the Scripture *doesn't* say the commands are easy to keep, or that they will fit seamlessly within our present culture, or that they won't ever make us feel uncomfortable. Instead, it says they aren't *burdensome*—unduly taxing. As all of God's commands, the command for Sabbath rest is ultimately for our good. For the flourishing of humankind. God gives us Sabbath because he loves us and we need it, and he commands it because without the command, we likely won't take it as seriously as our souls require. I'll be the first to admit that I've failed to give the day to God much more often than not. Sabbath isn't easy. But oh, it is good. And without stepping into Sabbath, our lives will always remain cluttered.

Accepting Rescue

I only dabbled in Sabbath practice until my first pastorate. It was there, in the rural windswept prairies of southern Wisconsin, that God first took me to Sabbath school. Sabbath practices began to stick at last, and not because ministry turned me holy but because the regular grind of church work wore away my strength. It wasn't that each day in the pastorate was too hard—some were quite difficult, of course, but others were easy, and most were simply normal days—it's that each one sapped a little bit of my vigor and resolve, and without a regular Sabbath, my physical and emotional and spiritual reserves were never properly refilled. I felt too important to take a full day off—I certainly *wasn't*, but I'd convinced myself no one could survive without me for a full twenty-four hours!—and after a couple years of being constantly on call, I began fantasizing about leaving ministry for good. I was too tired to follow God in the big things because I'd failed to accept his small, essential weekly gift.

It all started innocently enough. Our ministry setting couldn't have been more idyllic. A white, clapboard church on a country road. Farmland far and wide, corn and soybeans and an occasional herd of pigs or sheep. Daryl and I moved into the sprawling manse next door to the church—the parsonage owned by the congregation—and I finally began doing what I'd prayed about and trained for over the previous half-decade: preaching, teaching, visiting the sick, performing baptisms, officiating at weddings and funerals. Mostly I just spent time with the people from my congregation and the picturesque town that surrounded us. I watched the high school track meets, sat with youth and their parents at football games, stood with the veterans at the town parades, served at the local food pantry, hung around the town's diners for stories and laughs. I so desperately wanted to be good at it all. I was good at it. For a while.

No one tells you in seminary how slow the holy work of the church often is. It's much more like tending a garden or a vineyard than running a business. The work of God is a constant drip of water that wears away stony ground over decades. Rarely is it the bolt of lightning that breaks one apart in an instant. No one tells a brand-new pastor to pace herself. No one told me the importance of Sabbath (except God, of course), that neglecting it would not only put my soul at risk of burnout, but my congregation at risk of losing their pastor through no fault of their own.

But who had time to read the Bible devotionally when there were sermons to prepare? How was I supposed to make room for the slow seasoning of prayer when emergencies were, well, *emergent*? Sometimes the church basement flooded. Often the blizzards came. People were in and out of the hospital continually. After telling my Session (that's Presbyterian for "church governing board") at our very first meeting that I planned to take Fridays as a Sabbath, I then ignored my own words, habitually checking my email, answering my phone, and popping over to the church if I noticed a light burning. I worked fifty-five, then sixty, then seventy hours a week, not because the congregation demanded it but because I simply couldn't turn off. I was exhausted, and I had no one to blame but myself.

I fantasized about going back to school for a PhD—life in the academy seemed so easy compared to trying to keep my own scheduling boundaries in ministry. I dreamed about the day when Daryl could be a pastor or a full-time academic and I could do something—anything—else. One of the signs of burnout is increased snippiness, and as I neared the end of my rope, I became a one-woman sarcasm factory. Late one afternoon I responded churlishly to an email one of my board members sent me on a Friday.

"Courtney," she said, much more gently than my response deserved, "*I* can't keep your Sabbath for you."

She couldn't, of course. But I wasn't keeping it, either. We were at an impasse, God and me, and if I learned anything from seminary, it's that God tends to know best. Whether we like it or not, accept it or not, live into it or not, God loves us, understands us, and set the bounds of creation in place to bless us. But still, I struggled.

I wasn't designed to keep going forever, of course. You aren't either. Little moments here and there of rest and worship will not be enough to sustain us for the long road ahead. Whether you're in professional ministry or the business world, serving on the home front with tiny tots or in the armed forces with big tanks, God designed all of us to stop. There are no exceptions to the weekly call of Sabbath. Each of us is designed to need rest in order to keep going. Even our computers need to be powered down once in a while. As Anne Lamott so sagely put it, "Almost everything will work again if you unplug it for a few minutes, including you."[55]

It broke my heart to realize I might have to leave the church I loved when the congregation had done nothing but support and care for me, a pastor serving her very first church, as I learned the ins and outs of ministry. Some rural parishes are famous for being "pastor-killers," churches that are so conflictual they drive pastors out within months. This church was the opposite. They repainted the entire manse for us, remodeled its bathrooms, met us at the door with open arms. When I bungled a point of order in a meeting, my board secretary would come to my office a day or two later and say, ever so gently, "You probably didn't know this, but…" and humbly and kindly teach me what I needed to know. They trusted me with their burials and baptisms, at their hospital bedsides, and in bringing the word of God. They loved Daryl and me, and Lincoln when he came along, and we loved them too. And yet I was considering resigning. Because I hadn't stopped for one day a week, I was thinking about stopping for good. How many of our meltdowns might be prevented by accepting God's gift of regular, repeated, weekly rest?

Finally, the waters up to my neck, I realized God's rescue had been waiting in front of me the whole time. I didn't need to quit. What I needed was Sabbath.

Resurrecting an Ancient Practice

It's perhaps no surprise it took desperation for me to notice and grab hold of God's Sabbath rescue. The people of God have been walking away from its teaching and practice for millennia. It began with the Israelites, but the church today is no better. I can count on zero fingers the number of sermons I heard about it growing up, the number of lectures I heard on it in seminary. Daryl remembered only one, and that from when he was in junior high school. He still talks about it, because even as a thirteen-year-old it enticed him. It seemed so flat-out extreme. In the past twenty years or so, only a few thoughtful scholars—Marva Dawn, Walter Brueggemann, Eugene Peterson— have picked up the topic and also sought to live it out themselves. By and large the idea of practicing a true Sabbath has been treated as luxury at best and laziness at worst.

"Sabbath is okay for *some people*," the prevailing wisdom goes. "If they don't have *as much going on as we important people do*." That, my friends, is a load of horse manure. Sabbath has nothing to do with how high up we might be in our companies, our ministries, or our social circles. It is required of rich and poor alike, men and women, singles and marrieds. It's not about how much free time we can muster; it's about how faithful we want to be to our Lord, and how faithful he wants to teach us he is in return. If we take it only if it's convenient, it's not Sabbath.

Once we've realized we need this rest, this break, this soul-uncluttering day dedicated to worship and prayer, how do we begin? Following the Sabbath command is so out of the ordinary that we lack not only an understanding of what it is but a vocabulary for beginning to talk about it, too. It sounds antiquated to our modern ears; right up there with pantaloons and chignons and dying of consumption. Perhaps you, like me, grew up reading Laura Ingalls Wilder's Little House books. Her description of what she and her sisters were allowed to do on the Sabbath is forever etched into my memory because it sounds like the world's most tedious torture. In the morning, the whole family went to church. After that began the long afternoon in the parlor:

> They must sit quietly and listen while Ma read Bible stories to them, or stories about lions and tigers and white bears from Pa's big green book, *The Wonders of the Animal World.* They might look at pictures, and they might hold their rag dolls nicely and talk to them. But there was nothing else they could do.[56]

If this is keeping the Sabbath, please *do not sign me up.* But don't worry—Sabbath is better than this. So very, very much better.

Beginning with History

Since the Sabbath was first described in the Hebrew Scriptures, it is helpful to start with someone who knows that side of the story so well. Rabbi Abraham Heschel writes extensively on Sabbath practices, and he describes the day like this: "The Sabbath is a day for the sake of life.... It is not an interlude but the climax of living."[57] How incredibly counterintuitive this is! We think of Sabbath as an interruption; Heschel points to it as the apex of human existence. Put another way, the rest of human life—work and leisure and running a household and raising a family—are an interlude in returning to Sabbath, the great celebration of who God is and what God has done for us. Heschel writes of Sabbath as a holy and cosmic pause, an opportunity to commune with God as Adam and Eve did—in solitude, in worship, in nature, in rest. It is a respite from the everyday labors of life so that the soul can grow and heal and be restored. It is preparation for eternity.

Sabbath is an invitation to stop doing all the things we have to do—working and running errands and shuttling kids and answering emails and paying bills. We cannot and must not stop these things forever, or even for long, but we can stop almost everything for a single day, once a week. In this gracious, God-given pause, we invite God in. We fill the day with worship, with play, with family or friends or neighbors, with feasting, with naps. *Always* naps. (According to my grandpa, a Sunday afternoon nap is *the* secret to a victorious Christian life.) On the Sabbath, stop striving and trying and *doing* and sit in silence, play music, make art, cook slow food, and converse with those you love. At my house we build a lot of forts and read a lot of books. Most of all we stop running long enough to lift our eyes from our labors, noticing God, ourselves, and our neighbors again.

On the Sabbath day we remember anew what God has done for us—that the world is his, that the work is his. Often on the Sabbath Daryl and I notice things about our kids or our home or each other that had escaped our attention for days or weeks or months because it is only on Sabbath that we slow down enough to pay attention. Often we notice God's goodness to us—goodness that otherwise would have gone overlooked and without praise. This is perhaps even more important in seasons of joy and ease, when circumstance doesn't force us to rely on God in the same desperate way. Writes Brueggemann, "Moses is very big on remembering, because forgetting is a temptation in an affluent

> WE NEED REGULAR, RHYTHMIC REMINDERS OF GOD'S GOODNESS, OF THE PROPER PLACE OF OUR WORK AND THE PROPER PLACE OF OUR WORSHIP.

environment.... Sabbath is the break, regular and public, that permits us to remember."[58] We are, all of us, incredibly forgetful people. This is Heschel's point. This isn't forgetting something temporarily. It's forgetting that life and time are genuinely different than what we've convinced ourselves they *must* be like. We need regular, rhythmic reminders of God's goodness, of the proper place of our work and the proper place of our worship.

The most beautiful example of God's love for us and for Sabbath is that he loves both so much he took one himself, creating the world in six days and then resting on the seventh to enjoy his creation. According to Adele Calhoun, author of *The Spiritual Disciplines Handbook*:

> The Sabbath reminded people that they were finite. They could not constantly be on the go. There were limits to their energy. And to honor these limitations was to honor the infinite God, who himself worked and rested.[59]

If God, who is limitless, rested on the seventh day of his creative process, then perhaps we—who have definite limits—should, too. It isn't that God rested because he is God and could make up the time later. It's that *rest itself* is holy and God wanted to show us the way.

I can hear your protests. I've made them myself. There is work to be done. Money to be earned. Kids to be fed and clothed. Houses to tidy. Texts to return. Seven days are not *nearly* enough to get it all done; how on earth could we possibly do it all in *six*? It's fine for *God* to rest, he's *God*. He can create things out of nothing and rise from the dead, *of course* he can handle a six-day workweek. We mortals need every hour of every day and then some. Don't we?

Rabbi Heschel counters the argument that we won't have enough time by simply conceding it. It's true: we won't have enough time to do all we want to do, or even all we *need* to do. But perhaps that's not the point:

> Is it possible for a human being to do all his work in six days? Does not our work always remain incomplete? What the [Exodus 20 passage] means to convey is: Rest on the Sabbath as if all your work were done. Another interpretation: *Rest even from the thought of labor.*[60]

Sabbath is a weekly reminder that we will *never* finish all the work. We are finite creatures. Frail vessels. Limited beings. Some of our work will *always* remain undone. It doesn't matter if we sleep four hours a night like Elon Musk or listen to all our podcasts at double the speed like over-caffeinated graduate students. We *still* can't finish everything. God has designed the world that way. Sabbath gives us permission, once a week *every* week, to acknowledge these limits rather than trying to constantly push past them. This, my friends, is grace. It is gift.

As a mom of young children, the knowledge that I will have unfinished work when the Sabbath comes gives me both hope and a headache. I always believe I can get to the bottom of the laundry mountain *someday*, if I just try a *little* harder, but alas, I never do. Even if I had a full-time laundry service, it would never all be done because my boys are blueberry jam monsters who love to play in the dirt. But one of the graces of the Sabbath is not that we may rest from our labors because our labors are complete, but because God holds even the laundry in his mighty hands, and when we give it all back to him we begin to find ourselves in him again.

The Mechanics of Sabbath

So what does practicing the Sabbath look like? How can you or I keep the Sabbath holy without losing our jobs, alienating our families, or joining a cult? I'm so glad you asked, because if there's one gift I'd like to give *you*, it's to spare you the years of trial and error Daryl and I wasted trying to crack the code of Sabbath-keeping. We thought it was complicated. It isn't. It isn't *easy*—keeping the Sabbath, like any other spiritual discipline, takes time to learn—but it's incredibly simple. And God promises help each step of the way.

1. Preparing the Schedule

First, we prepare our schedules for a day of Sabbath rest. As Heschel's daughter, Susannah, notes, "Preparation for a holy day, my father often said, is as important as the day itself."[61] Without making a commitment in advance to keep the Sabbath, our time will naturally fill up with work and errands and chores and life. Scheduling Sabbath is the most challenging part for most people, Daryl and me included. It's hard to opt out of the rat race, even for a day. So we prepare our calendars, finding a day that we can regularly keep as a Sabbath. For most people this will be Sunday, the day that naturally holds worship and tends to have fewer outside commitments. Since Daryl and I are both in ministry and our boys aren't yet in school full-time, we take Fridays as our Sabbath. Starting next year, when our oldest is in kindergarten, we will take Friday afternoons through Saturday afternoons as Sabbath, following something closer to the Jewish rhythm of sundown to sundown.

We keep that day clear of all work commitments and log off of social media and email. We allow only praying and playing into the day. This doesn't mean the Sabbath is a day to entertain ourselves into oblivion with movies and television and laser tag, but it does mean we enter into playful pursuits that are particularly worshipful: taking the kids to the park, going on a hike, visiting the ocean. We make time for Jesus, opening the day in prayer and giving each person time to read Scripture, to journal, to pray. We create rather than consume, cooking and gardening and playing music rather than shopping and watching and listening to music. Sometimes we serve a neighbor in need or a friend who's struggling. We always nap.

> SABBATH IS TIMELESS; IT IS FOR EVERY PLACE, EVERY GENERATION, EVERY BELIEVER.

After we learned, at long last, how to keep a Sabbath at my first pastorate, we moved across the country to California to a bigger church, a faster-paced area, and a higher cost of living. The church ordained Daryl into the ministry as well, and suddenly we were a two-pastor family. We quickly fell back into old habits. I spent my Sabbaths grading papers and answering emails once again; Daryl popped over to the church for "just a minute" and ended up staying for hours. Suddenly we needed to relearn Sabbath. But we soon found that our excuses for ignoring the fourth commandment held up just as well in California as they did in Wisconsin: not at all. Sabbath is timeless; it is for every place, every generation, every believer. We stepped into Sabbath fully once again.

When your calendar changes or your kids grow, you may need to refresh your Sabbath commitment, too. One pastor I know sat down with his wife to figure out how to keep the Lord's day and realized that in order to do it, every single member of their household would have to give up something they loved—a sports practice, a music lesson, a side hustle—in order to keep it. Yet they did it, and it changed their family from the inside out.

Do Daryl and I sometimes schedule things on Fridays? Yes, sometimes we do. If a congregant dies and Friday is the only day that works for the funeral, we will do that. Jesus healed on the Sabbath, after all. He was faithful in it, not rigid or ridiculous. We visit folks in the hospital who are near death. Occasionally I've even taken a speaking engagement on a Friday, but only when we are certain we can make up the hours by taking another day as our Sabbath. The key is to have these exceptions be truly rare. Fifty weeks out of the year, our Fridays are sacred Sabbaths; but when God puts something truly unexpected on our plates, we trust him with that, too.

Some of you have crazy work schedules or keep several jobs to make ends meet. I've been there. To be honest, I *am* there. And parents and caregivers *never* get a day off easily, Sabbath or no. If any of those describes you, I'd encourage you to find even a small Sabbath.

Ask your spouse to give you half a day to yourself, and then return the favor. Call the deacons or the elders at your church and ask if they can sit with your aging grandfather while you go for a walk and feel the breeze on your face. Take the money you saved for a rainy day and spend it on a relief pitcher—an aide or a nanny or a babysitter or a nurse or a house cleaner—for even an hour or two. Be honest with your parents or your small group or your lovely next-door neighbor about what a blessing it would be to have a night away from the kids, and then take them up on their offer to host a sleepover. Ask Jesus to help—he's in the Sabbath business. Be creative—even a small, weekly Sabbath is eons more restorative and faithful than nothing at all.

2. Preparing the Space

After we've prepared our schedule, we prepare our home. If you're anything like us, by the end of the workweek your living space looks very...lived-in. I'm talking "no one has taken out the recycling in six days and the kitchen counter is now sparkling-water-can-Everest" lived-in. Sometimes I find an apple core the toddler stashed behind the couch last Friday. By Thursday even our fridge has given up, and week-old dinner leftovers threaten us with their powerful tentacles every time we crack open the door. There are backpacks and work satchels and books and laundry and dishes strewn far and wide because we try to be tidy but by Thursday night—the last day of our workweek, which, because of Daryl's Bible study and the College & Young Adults group I lead concurrently, ends around 10 p.m.—we are *done*. Exhausted. Spent. Running on fumes.

But—thanks be to God!—Sabbath is coming. Once again. Every week. And with Sabbath comes rest. So Daryl and I pour ourselves a glass of something (I'm a ginger ale girl, he's a wine guy—you can tell which one of us was raised in California) and we spend half an hour readying the house for Sabbath. It won't be mom-is-coming-to-visit-clean (I *know* you check the microwave, Mom), but it will welcome us into the next day with peace. We tidy the big things, throw the toys into bins (it helps that there are both fewer toys *and* fewer bins these days), pile laundry out of sight, clean up the kitchen, and collapse together in bed. We offer our Thursday evening babysitter a few extra bucks if she does any cleaning, and those are dollars *well* spent. I check the freezer for food that I can throw in the crock pot in the early afternoon the next day, and double-check we are stocked with donuts because on Sabbath our sons get two things they crave all week long: sugary breakfast treats and uninterrupted attention from both Mom and Dad.

Perhaps you want to light a candle or read a Scripture to start your Sabbath day with intention. Maybe you, like us, want to dedicate an out-of-reach spot for your cell phones and other screens so you don't have to rely on willpower to stay off of them on Sabbaths. However you prepare your space, make it a place that will feel restful and special to you, set apart for this special and holy and celebratory day.

3. Preparing the Soul

Finally, we are called by God to prepare *ourselves* for Sabbath. If you're going to begin Sabbath practices for the first time, know that they sound good on paper, but there is a bit of a learning curve. Your first few Sabbaths might be painful. Doing less will be difficult after a lifetime doing more and more and more. Pain signals the beginning of healing. We've trained ourselves to run so fast and so hard that slowing down is a new skill to learn. It'll take practice. Yet, as Tim Kreider

> IF WE HAVE GIVEN IN TO IT, WE CAN ALSO DECIDE TO KICK IT OUT.

notes, "The present hysteria is not a necessary or inevitable condition of life; it's something we've chosen, if only by our acquiescence to it."[62] If we have given in to it, we can also decide to kick it out. Sabbath will teach this lesson, if we let it.

Prepare yourself in prayer—tell God that you are giving him the day. If you're the only Sabbath practitioner in your home—and it may take you a while to convert even faithful Christians within your household to this radical ancient command—think through which elements of worship, play, celebration, and rest would most nurture you and draw you closer to Jesus. Communal worship—church—adorns Sabbath beautifully. If you have little kids as I do, a few storybooks may be in order. Maybe you're an adrenaline junkie and you need a few hours on a mountain bike or a surfboard to feel close to God. Think about how you celebrate best. Our kids get donuts. I get my weekly Dr. Pepper, and I enjoy *every* drop of that sweet, sweet goodness. My extraverted friends need lots of social time on their Sabbaths. Our introverted family usually spends the bulk of Sabbath with each other or alone, and just an hour or two welcoming friends for dinner or visiting neighbors.

As you prepare your soul, begin to enter into the slowness of Sabbath. Try to turn off the screens a bit before bed so you can begin to let down into a rest that can never be digitized. The soul preparation continues into the morning of the day itself when you step into a different way of being—one that is not rushed, but grounded; not hurried, but at peace. What really marks Sabbath morning within the four walls of our home is that no one is in a rush. I'm not trying to get the preschooler dressed while shoveling pancakes into the toddler. Daryl isn't digging around for a missing dress shoe while typing out an email with one hand. No one utters the words, "Hurry up," or "We're going to be late," or "How can a human person possibly take that long to poop?"

Sabbath mornings are slow. If you aren't a pastor and your Sabbath morning includes worship, consider going to a service that starts later in the day so you don't have the fire drill of trying to find little girls' tights and teenage boys' polo shirts and the flatiron that you only use once a week. Our Catholic neighbors—an incredibly kind and creative family of eight—purposefully choose to attend an early afternoon Mass on Sundays because, as the father once told Daryl, "If you go to church at 12:30, there's not a lot you can do before, and there's not a lot you can do after. It helps us keep the Sabbath." Preach.

Once you've prepared your schedule, your space, and your soul, lean into the goodness of Sabbath. Drink it up.

Praying and Playing

When Sabbath arrives, in all its glory and simplicity and joy, my first response is almost always, "Meh." Not what you were expecting? The hardest part of Sabbath-keeping for me is those first few hours. I can't *work* at Sabbath. I can't be *good* at it or excel at it or do it *right*. That motor runs hard in many of us, so don't be surprised if you feel unmoored for a bit.

Don't be surprised if you have a few minutes or even hours where you feel like Sabbath is pointless and horrible and the stress of the week comes crashing down around your head. That is exactly what happens when the cortisol- and adrenaline-fueled stress that carries us through our frantic lives begins to wear off, and we can actually feel the things we're feeling. Barbara Brown Taylor calls this particular ennui "Sabbath sickness." As she puts it:

> Anyone who practices Sabbath for even an afternoon usually suffers a little spell of Sabbath sickness. Try it and you too may be amazed by how quickly your welcome rest begins to feel like something closer to a bad cold. Okay, that was nice. Okay, you are ready to go back to work now.[63]

This is normal. Expect it, name it for what it is, surrender it to Jesus, and let it pass. It nearly always will.

Resist the temptation to turn on the news, check your phone, or dive into a work project. Instead, look out the window. Really taste your breakfast. Look into the faces of those in your home. Putter around. Read a book. Take a walk. Do nothing productive, as a radical exercise of faith in the one who has done it all for you.

In times of joy, Daryl and the kids and I have found

even greater wells of it on the Sabbath, celebrating the time we have to drink in the excitement of a move, a graduation, a milestone, a birthday. In seasons of suffering, Sabbath has anchored us to the rock of Jesus Christ, reminding us that he is and will be with us in the storm. Marva Dawn, the great Sabbath-practitioner and author of *Keeping the Sabbath Wholly*, put it this way: "The greatest result of Sabbath resting is the opportunity to know the presence of God, no matter what our present circumstances might be."[64] We've found this to be true. I'm willing to bet that you will, too.

As we reveled in the gift of Sabbath, finally accepting what God had wanted for us for years and years, he turned our gaze to the most terrifying horizon yet. Sabbath isn't just for us—it's for the world. With our newfound Sabbath freedom, God was ready to help us discover every introvert's worst nightmare: *hospitality.*

Hospitality

HOT DOGS, STRANGERS, AND YOU

Somewhere is better than anywhere.
–Flannery O'Connor

There are a lot of reasons *not* to practice hospitality. I have a whole list of them myself. Daryl and I work, our house is often a mess, the kids are chaos incarnate when we have guests over, people sometimes have needs we aren't prepared to meet, I'm an introvert, I'm an introvert, I'm an introvert, I'm an introvert. You might have a list of your own.

The age of social media makes these pressures even worse. Daryl and I married a few years before the diabolical photo-and-craft-sharing website known as Pinterest came on the scene, and for that I'll always be grateful. We used evergreen branches to decorate the tables and purchased matching fleeces for bridesmaid gifts (we got married in Wisconsin in January, so...

yeah). If we'd married even a few years later, I would have felt ALLTHEPRESSURE to decorate with snow-frosted princess pine dipped in a sherry glaze and covered with environmentally friendly glitter, or some such nonsense. Practicing hospitality in the age of social media can feel like inviting a James Beard Award-winning chef over and serving him cheap ramen. Are these fish sticks *locally sourced*?

You might even think that inviting people into our lives—with all their mess and chaos and ways of being not *quite* as great as we are—is the opposite of un-cluttering. Whenever we hosted overnight guests in our little two-bedroom condo, everyone involved spent lots of time tripping over suitcases and air mattresses and feeling generally quite cluttered. But part of the reason Daryl and I started on this uncluttered journey to begin with was because God was calling us to a life of deeper fellowship with him. And God is quite serious about hospitality. And if you say no to the call of God in your life, sometimes you end up in the belly of a big fish (just ask Jonah). Still, I protested.

PRACTICING HOSPITALITY IN THE AGE OF SOCIAL MEDIA CAN FEEL LIKE INVITING A JAMES BEARD AWARD-WINNING CHEF OVER AND SERVING HIM CHEAP RAMEN.

Yet in all my protestations—*I can't be hospitable, I don't know how to cook anything but boxed pasta, our house is never tidy, etc. etc. ETC.*—it occurred to me that I wasn't even exactly sure what Christian hospitality *was*. I knew it was a spiritual practice, and one Jesus talked quite a lot about. But was Jesus really expecting me to have a museum-tidy living room? Was Christian hospitality something I needed to take cooking classes to be able to fully enter into? And was this spiritual practice synonymous with women's brunches where well-meaning ladies spent countless hours crafting centerpieces? Because *that was officially not my jam.* I'd rather lead a junior high overnight with unlimited buckets of Mountain Dew and a dodgeball tournament than make a single centerpiece. Whatever that table beautification gene is, I do not possess it.

So there I was, feeling paralyzed and frustrated and terrified that God was going to call me into the adult, Christian version of home economics class, where I'd have to finally learn the difference between a muffin and a scone, when Daryl reminded me of the story we heard when we were undergraduates. A chapel speaker told us she and her husband wanted to open the doors of their home to friends and strangers alike, so they started a weekly dinner. "Our Sunday night dinner is open to anyone," she said. "But it's not about the food. In fact, we serve the same thing every time. It's cost-effective, and most people like it. We boil hot dogs." This still horrifies Daryl. According to him, "Hot dogs are fine, but you have to grill them." Still, remembering the simplicity of their offering inspired me. It freed me. Perhaps I'd been believing untruths about hospitality all this time.

Hospitality Myth-Busting

The more I dug into Scripture, the more I realized I'd come to believe a couple of particularly harmful myths about this ancient practice. First, I'd come to believe that hospitality was a domestic virtue, mainly concerned with an impressive dinner spread, perfectly polished furniture, and exceedingly well-behaved children. This is miles from its biblical definition. Take the Levitical command, for example: "When a foreigner resides among you in your land, do not mistreat them. The foreigner residing among you must be treated as your native-born. Love them as yourself, for you were foreigners in Egypt."[65] The home front isn't even mentioned in this passage; instead it's about the treatment of the outsider, the stranger, the newcomers in our midst.

Though hospitality is about making outsiders feel at home, it is much more a *heart* issue than a *house* issue. We can practice it in any space, public or private. Buying coffee for a cold stranger at a neighborhood diner is as hospitable as hosting a dinner party. Maybe even more so. Will there be times God asks us to open our houses and set a few more places at our tables? Of course. And in those moments we must not let a laundry list of excuses about throw pillows or seasonal ornamentation or how long it's been since we've vacuumed keep us from listening to God about whom he's calling us to love right now, in this moment. But hospitality is first about the heart.

Uncoupling hospitality from a purely domestic sphere can actually free us to make our private spaces *more* available to God, because suddenly being hospitable is about God and another person, not about us. This tackles the second myth I'd come to believe: that hospitality was somehow about *me*, the giver. It was something I had to *do*. I believed that in order to be hospitable, I needed to grow in certain skills: homemaking ability, culinary acumen, and probably guest bedroom decorating (unless accenting with Dr. Seuss books, unopened boxes of baby wipes, and stray socks is the epitome of chic, in which case, I *already* excel in this area). But making hospitality about us misses the point, too. If we are inviting friends over to gaze upon our guitar collection, our first-edition hardback books signed by the author, or an amazing new playroom organizational system—we aren't practicing hospitality, but vanity.

Welcoming the Stranger

Christian hospitality is an extension of God's hospitality to us—the ways he constantly and continually makes space for us to be seen and heard, valued and loved. It is, as Elizabeth Newman notes in her book *Untamed Hospitality*, "being with," not "doing for."[66] It isn't about a perfect chocolate soufflé; it's about seeing the weariness in another's eyes. It isn't about a living room free from laundry baskets (and good thing, too, for that is where ours reside 98 percent of the time); it's about making clear to the neighbor, the friend, the stranger, that there is room for *them*. In the practice of hospitality, God allows us to create a kind of Sabbath for the other, welcoming them as God welcomes us.

There's a scene in the novel *Babbitt* by Sinclair Lewis where George Babbitt and his wife Myra invite a married couple of a slightly lower status over for dinner. The visiting husband and wife make several social faux pas, and the Babbitts titter together later about how daft the couple appeared within the confines of their chic middle-class home. Then George is invited to a dinner party thrown by his boss. He and Myra agonize over what to wear, how to act, what to say. They attend the party—which is at a later hour than they are accustomed to dining—and do their best to fit in. They fail in subtle and heartbreaking ways. Hospitality, Lewis infers, is never a level playing field.

And yet, according to Jesus, that's exactly the point. Hospitality isn't about reciprocation or making a good impression or finding a social equal—it's about loving those who need to be loved. Foreigners, neighbors, and friends alike, with an emphasis on loving the stranger. In Luke 14, Jesus attends a dinner party thrown by a Pharisee. Witnessing the higher-ups quibble over who should sit where in order to receive the most honor, he tells them, "When you give a banquet, invite the poor, the crippled, the lame, the blind, and you will be blessed. Although they cannot repay you, you will be repaid."[67] God's focus is on reaching out and gathering in, so everyone may hear of his love and experience his grace. Hospitality is never about status or position, impressing our neighbors or outdoing our friends.

Stories of hospitality are found on nearly every page of Scripture. Whether it was Abraham inviting in the strangers who passed by his tent, Jesus visiting with a woman at the well, or Paul relying on the love of his church plants to provide him with meals in prison, stories of people making space for one another, caring for one another, and inviting each other in because of what God has done for them abound. There's Peter's reminder that we must "Offer hospitality to one another without grumbling."[68] There's Paul's command that we "Share with the Lord's people who are in need. Practice hospitality."[69] Perhaps there is no single way we walk more faithfully in the footsteps of Jesus than when we do just that.

The Mechanics of Hospitality

So how, then, do we practice hospitality? An international industry has sprung up around it—fluffy white towels and catered dinners and cruise ships galore. Yet pay-to-play hospitality misses the point. Christian hospitality is always free. Come as you are. Come sit and enjoy. Come be heard and seen and loved. We all too easily clutter up the possibilities for hospitality with obstacles God never intends for us. Jesus' point is that hospitality is tested in the spontaneous need of our neighbor. When they are tired, sick, wounded, or stressed, are we willing to make room?

At its heart, Christian hospitality is simply making space for another. If we have willingness, time, and space, we can be hospitable. And if we are simply willing, we will find the time and the space. If that sounds small, it's because it is. As Newman notes, "The faithful practice of hospitality must begin (and also end) with what our society will tend to regard as

> HOSPITALITY IS TESTED IN THE SPONTANEOUS NEED OF OUR NEIGHBOR. WHEN THEY ARE TIRED, SICK, WOUNDED, OR STRESSED, ARE WE WILLING TO MAKE ROOM?

of little consequence. Waiting for the earthshaking event or the cultural or even ecclesial revolution can paralyze us. We are rather, as the gospel reminds us, called to be faithful in the small things."[70]

This entire uncluttered journey centers on small things, on the belief that God cares about not only sparrows but socks, not just the lilies of the field but the leftovers in the fridge. The invitation, instruction, and command to practice hospitality is much the same. We don't need to sell our house and invest in a bed and breakfast; we do need to begin to say yes to the small ways God wants to make us more like Jesus by calling us to reach out to others in love. Jesus eats with tax collectors and "sinners," showing them that they have a place in God's kingdom. He welcomes women and children, making space for those society pushed to the outside. He even loves a good dinner party, reclining with John—his closest friend—more than once to enjoy a good feast. Jesus makes space for others; so can we. So must we.

A Two-Way Table

Sometimes making space for others will mean accepting their hospitality, too. Christians are, by and large, pretty terrible about this. We want to give, never receive. It's striking that the hospitality of Jesus—our model and guide—is regularly two-sided. He doesn't just give hospitality; he receives it, and in doing so he helps us remember that hospitality is about relationship. When Mary washes his feet with perfume, he sits and receives.[71] When Zacchaeus's hard, lonely, extortionist exterior begins to crack, Jesus proclaims to the crowd that he will be dining at the man's house that very day.[72] Because hospitality isn't *doing for*, it's *being with*, we will find ourselves on the receiving end as well as the giving end, and when God places us in the seat of the receiver, we must learn to open our hearts and our hands. It may be "more blessed to give than to receive,"[73] but woe to the one who is too proud to receive, for we are all receivers first. Perhaps nowhere is this illustrated as beautifully as it is in the story of Mary and Martha.

Martha gets kind of a bad rap in Scripture. *Someone* has to feed Jesus; he's a guest in her home, after all. It seemed far easier to be Mary, sitting at his feet while Martha tried to hunt down a chicken to pluck and some potatoes to peel. Yet how many of us need Jesus' reminder to Martha on a daily basis?

"Martha, dear Martha," Jesus says, as her frustration bubbles over. Her sister, Mary, sits at Jesus' feet as she—and only she!—struggles to figure out how to extend proper hospitality to this last-minute addition to their dinner table. "Dear Martha, you're fussing far too much and getting yourself worked up over nothing. One thing only is essential, and Mary has chosen it—it's the main course, and won't be taken from her."[74] I love that this Scripture translation leans on a food metaphor. Doubtless Martha is slaving in the kitchen, but Jesus wants her to know that food is secondary to being with him. Dinner would get done—perhaps, once Jesus was finished, they could prepare it together. But this moment with him was *the moment*, the one that could order all the others into their proper spheres. The hospitality was in the *being with*, not the *doing for*. It was in the small, sacred gesture of sitting and listening, receiving from Jesus, not first in the gesture of food preparation.

The Freedom of Simple Hospitality

Hospitality needn't be expensive or fancy—and in fact, sometimes when it is, it can make our guests feel even less at ease. I feel much more at home on a couch that looks like people can sit on it than one that looks showroom-pristine, don't you? One of my college professors and her husband opened their home weekly to students, clergy, and visiting scholars alike. Their home was beautiful but clearly lived-in, and each week they served simple, hearty soup. Most of my fellow students and I weren't at risk of going

> THE HOSPITALITY WAS IN THE SMALL, SACRED GESTURE OF SITTING AND LISTENING, RECEIVING FROM JESUS.

hungry, but at age nineteen and twenty and twenty-one, away from home for the first time, we were starving for something else—adults willing to pour into us, to answer questions about faith, to live the Christian life alongside us as mentors and guides and friends.

I showed up at that dinner more than once in a pretty ragged spiritual state, and each time there were stacks of bowls and spoons, a place for me to sit, and people willing to let me ask all the questions my heart held. Once I sat between a brilliant endowed chair of the college and a missionary to a closed country who'd just survived another attempt on his life. They talked, in a totally casual and normal way, about following Jesus no matter the cost. Witnessing their conversation fanned sparks of faith in my own heart that burn to this day. I never once noticed whether the baseboards of that home were dusted, but I sure felt loved by being invited in.

When Daryl and I moved into our house this year, we purchased a photo of two tattered ships to hang on our living room wall. The ships are in a dry harbor. The tide has gone out; a storm is just receding. One leans on the other as the sun sets. It's a visual representation of what we want not only our home but our lives to be—a port in the storm for those who have been battered by the waves. The more we uncluttered our possessions and our schedules, the more God began to open up space for hospitality in our spirits. We started to notice those who needed a harbor to rest in, for a meal or an evening or a day. Now that our schedule wasn't maxed out to the gills, we more easily tuned in to those he placed in our path. Hospitality became an extension of two less cluttered souls. My prayer is that this will become true for you, too. The world is hungry for genuine Christian hospitality, a soft landing place in a cactus culture.

If I'm completely honest, I still have my laundry list of excuses as to why I'd rather not practice hospitality. There are days I choose self over neighbor, comfort over love, media over conversation. There are days I hide when the doorbell rings because introverts *need ten minutes' notice to gear up for other humans, thank you very much.* Very few people have the unwavering, spirit-filled gift of hospitality, but those of us who aren't particularly gifted in it (myself very much included) are in no way excluded from the biblical mandate to welcome the stranger. I'm learning, and God is a faithful and patient teacher.

As we create room for God and our hearts become more like his, our desire to be hospitable to the friend, the neighbor, and the stranger will grow and grow. And that's one thing that can get as big as the sky, without creating a *speck* more clutter.

Hot dogs, anyone?

10

Listening and Speaking

HOLY WHISPERS

Being unmade, we are remade
and given back to ourselves.
–Jackson Clelland

I could frequently use a divine two-by-four to the noggin to get my attention, rather than a soft tap on the shoulder. Yet as I've uncluttered, I've found listening to God's still, small voice becoming far, far easier.

As space and silence open up in your life, what can you hear that you couldn't before? As my life became quieter, I was shocked by all the previously unnoticed things I could hear. Our appliances hummed. My heart beat. (Thank goodness.) A car alarm went off several streets over. Without the constant rush and clamor of podcasts and Pandora, frenetic activity and fast-paced scheduling, for the first time in decades I could *hear*. And not just ambient noise, either. I could hear myself. I could hear my kids. I could hear God. I'm willing to bet you've begun to hear more, too.

One of my favorite Bible stories is that of Elijah. There's a ton packed into his life—ravens bringing bread, fire from heaven, the parting of a river's water, pagan priests and power-hungry kings and vengeful queens. It's a real adventure story, a Star Wars-like epic with twists and turns and villains and heroes and moments of true humanity. One such human moment is in 1 Kings 19, when Elijah is on the run for his life. He's had a hard road so far, as is true of every prophet, and he's tired and worn down and discouraged and raw. So when Queen Jezebel—she of the bouts of murderous rage—sends him a message saying, "I'm going to kill you tomorrow, just see if I don't," his strength fails, and he sits down under a bush, praying for God to end his suffering.

> WITHOUT THE CONSTANT RUSH AND CLAMOR OF PODCASTS AND PANDORA, FRENETIC ACTIVITY AND FAST-PACED SCHEDULING, FOR THE FIRST TIME IN DECADES I COULD *HEAR*.

"I have had enough, LORD," he says. "Take my life."[75] I love how honest the Scriptures are with Elijah's discouragement. This isn't a tired pastor asking her board politely for a sabbatical. It isn't an overworked parent asking his wife for a little alone time to recharge. Elijah is asking to *die*. He's *that* over it. And as he waits for God to come and *do something*, as so often happens to each of us when we reach our end, he falls asleep.

An angel comes to him, gently rouses him, and offers him food and water. God knows that, as Vince Lombardi once said, "Fatigue makes cowards of us all," and he cares for Elijah's physical needs first. Elijah's strength (if not his heart) restored, he naps a bit more, eats a bit more, and then wearily but willingly follows God up to the slopes of Mount Horeb. If he has to keep going, at least God has given him a full belly and a night's rest.

On the mountain, Elijah lays out his complaint. The people he's called to serve have turned their backs on the Almighty. They've trampled upon God's promises, torn down his places of worship, killed his other prophets, and now they're after Elijah, too. What, he wants to know, is the point of any of it? Why should he keep following God when things are just so hard?

As so often happens in Scripture, God answers Elijah not with a solution but with an invitation: "Go out," God says, "and stand on the mountain in the presence of the Lord, for the Lord is about to pass by."

Elijah obeys. What does he have to lose, after all? It's this or death. As he stands on the mountain, a series of loud, intense events begins. First there's a wind so strong rocks are torn apart. Can you imagine the sound of rocks splitting? I grew up on the edge of a northern lake, and in the spring when the ice would melt, its cracks and groans were so loud they'd wake my family from sleep. "But," the Scripture says, "the LORD was not in the wind." Then there is a great earthquake, and Elijah feels the mountain trembling beneath his feet, the very ground under him giving way. But the Lord is not found there either. After the earthquake, there is a hot, raging, consuming fire. Can you feel its warmth? Its power? Can you hear its roar? But the Lord is not in even this mighty inferno.

Finally, after all of these shows of force have blown and shaken and burned themselves out, there is absolute silence. Absolute stillness. Can you hear it? In this silence comes a gentle whisper. Here, of course, is God. "When Elijah heard it, he pulled his cloak over his face and went out and stood at the mouth of the cave."[76] There, God meets him. There, God ministers to him. Once Elijah waits out the noise, he hears God speak. When we quiet ourselves, we just might hear him, too.

We're well over halfway through the *Uncluttered* journey, and my hope for you is that the noise in your life has begun to die down. That with less clutter and fewer events, you've begun to discover space in your home and your schedule and your soul to hear from God, for God often speaks softly. He is quite polite that way. He doesn't shout or cajole or yell. God's voice is the gentle whisper. He waits for silences in which he can be heard.

Dashboard Confessional

The whispers first showed up for me in the silences in my car. Not audible whispers, of course, but nudges. Reminders. Graces. I'd be driving with a podcast going or NPR or a CD, and suddenly I'd realize I was missing a chance to talk to Jesus. I'd turn off the music—even worship music is sometimes just distracting noise—and drive, watching the palm trees in the California winds, the other drivers in their SUVs and beat-up sedans and flashy vanity vehicles. My mind would wander, and God would work.

Remember how much I love you?

His words surprised me. God almost always greets us first with words of courage or kindness. *Do not fear. I am with you. You are mine.* Even when we sin—which is every single day of our lives—God usually begins calling us back with words of invitation, not condemnation. Like God met Elijah on the mountain, weary and wounded, to minister to him with love and nourishment, God met me in the quiet space between the driver's seat and the dashboard. He was there all along, but I'd been too busy to notice, to dial in, to hear. As you seek a simpler way, are you beginning to find yourself showing up in your own story? Being present in your own life? Are you starting to hear God's voice more clearly?

Listening to God—besides the odd road-to-Damascus or burning-bush scenario where God makes himself known in a bright, attention-grabbing flash—is a skill like any other. It can be cultivated, strengthened, honed, and focused. Like any other spiritual practice, it can be learned. So how do we take some of our newly created space and let God refresh our souls with it?

God Breezes All Around

First, we tune in. At the first church I pastored, there was this great lady named Peg. Peg lived a simple life. She resided in the same town of three thousand people for seven decades. She raised kids and grandkids and foster kids. She cleaned houses for a living and served our church as a deacon, taking meals to shut-ins, bringing communion to those in assisted-living facilities, and visiting people in the nearby hospital. She also called me at the church office nearly every week with good news.

"Pastor!" she'd chirp. "I just had to tell you what happened to me today. It was *such* a God-breeze!" A God-breeze was Peg's shorthand for a moment she'd noticed God at work. Some of these instances were deeply profound (the mending of an estranged relationship) while others were incredibly simple (a crocus blooming as a sign spring was on its way). Peg noticed God at work everywhere. But then, Peg was *listening* for God everywhere. She could have easily grown bitter from years of backbreaking work scrubbing floors; instead, she couldn't wait to share with me and the rest of the congregation the way God blessed her with an unexpected phone call from an old friend.

In the wee hours one summer morning, Peg died. Her death was sudden. Unexpected. Losing her rattled us all. Until she died, she hadn't even been sick. As I met with her family to plan her memorial service, I found myself wrestling with what her loss meant for me, too. Not only was she a pillar in the church, she was a friend. Who would remind me of God at work all around if Peg wasn't calling anymore? Then I realized she'd been training our whole congregation for decades in how to see God the way she did. Her life was a lighthouse, shining with a light not her own. Peg could see God at work everywhere because she looked for him everywhere. Couldn't I do the same? Can't we all?

Between Elijah on the mountain and Peg on the farmlands, I've learned I must tune in. If I believe God is at work in the world, then I can prepare to notice him wherever I go, from my house, to the grocery store, to the church, to the doctor's office, to the playground, to the traffic jam. An uncluttered mind—freed from digital distraction, unhealthy preoccupation with possessions, and an overburdened schedule—will begin to awaken to spiritual realities all around.

I took an animal tracking course back in junior high school. (I was homeschooled in rural Wisconsin, which meant I could identify every kind of tree within a fifty mile radius but didn't learn how to put on mascara until I was in my twenties. True story.) The instructors taught us to notice things we'd usually pass by without a second look. Snapped twigs. Broken leaves. Indentations in the soil. Animal poop. (That part was a *big* hit with the middle school boys.) After a few lessons, I couldn't walk a step into the woods and *not* notice these things. I was Daniel Boone out on the frontier; my eyes had been opened to a previously unseen reality. Animals left evidence *everywhere*! They always had; I just hadn't noticed. Our ability to sense God at work can be honed in a similar way.

This doesn't mean we have our heads perpetually in the clouds. On the contrary, paying more attention to unseen spiritual realities should also put us ever more in touch with what's tangible, visible, and right in front of us. It should deepen our interest in science, music, food, nature, politics, the news, and other cultures. God is profoundly practical. He created the physical world, after all, from its animals and plants to its chemistry and physics, creating us to need food and water and shelter and community. God is profoundly interested in both our bodies and our souls. N. T. Wright puts it this way: "With the incarnation itself being the obvious and supreme example, and the gospel sacraments of baptism and Eucharist not far behind, one can learn to discover the presence of God not only *in* the world, as though by a fortunate accident, but *through* the world."[77] Don't wait for Sunday worship to look for God. He's between you and the pages of this book right now, too.

In practicing the expectation that God is in and through and all around, we will begin to meet God in the in-between places of life. While patience is a fruit of the spirit, the Christian life is one of hope and anticipation, too. It isn't just all sitting back and waiting to receive from God. It's also crying out over injustice, stepping up in service, understanding the immediacy of the needs of our neighbors. As Tish Harrison Warren writes in *The Liturgy of the Ordinary*, "Christians are marked not only by patience, but also by longing."[78] Or as T. S. Eliot put it, "This is the time of tension, between dying and birth."[79] And God is there.

As I've continued to unclutter my space and my schedule and my soul, I've found myself in these in-between places more often. I used to fill every moment I waited in a grocery line with social media browsing, every silence in my car with the radio, every evening with a couple episodes of something or other from Netflix. But now, in these moments between an appointment and the house, between choosing produce and purchasing it, between asking a question and receiving an answer, between getting into bed and falling asleep, I have learned to listen for God. He's always been present, but it is only now I am learning to hear.

> IN PRACTICING THE EXPECTATION THAT GOD IS IN AND THROUGH AND ALL AROUND, WE WILL BEGIN TO MEET GOD IN THE IN-BETWEEN PLACES OF LIFE.

The Listening Lord

Not only do we hear from God when we carve out more space and silence, but God waits to hear from us, too, inviting us to share our hearts with him day by day, hour by hour. Paul encourages us to "pray continually,"[80] not in a rush of wordy paragraphs but in a relationship that holds nothing back from the one who loves us. This is how Elijah's journey began. He asked God to end his life. This is a legitimate, honest, heartfelt prayer. I think if we're truthful, most of us have been there a time or two, asking God what the point of any of this is. A friend once shared with me that a few months after her divorce, she simply lay down on her bed and asked God to take her.

"He didn't," she said. "So I had to get up and ask him what to do next."

God invites us to speak to him about everything in our lives and on our hearts, sharing it all with him, whether in lament or in songs of joy. I love how James puts it: "Is anyone among you in trouble? Let them pray. Is anyone happy? Let them sing songs of praise."[81] Prayer need not be more complicated than this. Words given to God while we sit in traffic. Songs sung when our hearts overflow with excitement. Feet pounding the pavement when we need to run out our anger with God. God's holy whispers often come in response to our most heartfelt cries.

Kids are great at this. My preschooler can't wait to tell me all about his day. Most of it wouldn't register on an adult's scale of "worthy of repeating," but the cat he saw across the street, the neighbor who lent him his scooter, the Goldfish crackers Dad bought—

these things matter to him. And you'd better believe they matter to God. Lincoln doesn't censor himself when he shares his day with me, because he trusts wholeheartedly that I love hearing about the scooter and the cat and the crackers. And now that I'm uncluttered enough to hear the care in his voice and see the excitement in his eyes, I genuinely do. Almost all the time.

Holy whispers abound when we begin conversing with God on a daily, hourly, minute-by-minute basis, bringing him into our struggles, offering up our sadness, remembering that he is the source of all our joy. Lincoln went through a phase where he'd stop mid-play and yell out, "Thank you, God!" It wasn't something he'd seen modeled by his pastor-parents; he just somehow knew that his joy came from the Lord of life, and he wanted to give thanks.

In a world of more and more noise, of fires and earth-quakes, winds and floods, the same God who whispered to Elijah is whispering to you, to me, to your neighbor, and to the world he loves. He speaks, and he wants to hear your voice, too. What a God. What a gift. Let us tune in and talk back, reveling in holy whispers that will grow easier to hear as our ears become ever more attuned.

Uncluttered Kids

SIMPLE, SOULFUL PARENTING

Let the little children come to me,
and do not hinder them.

−Jesus

I am no parenting expert. Anyone who knows me is already laughing because it is so obvious that is true. I have called Cheetos a vegetable (they *are* made from corn...), stared at my phone without noticing the toddler is putting pebbles in his ear, and let my kids wear whatever they want out of the house, including galoshes on 110-degree days. My husband once heard me tell our preschooler that after 8 p.m. "I don't have to be nice anymore. It's in my contract." Our kids rarely remember to shield their sneezes from spraying whoever's near. Daryl and I honestly prefer reading books alone to letting the kids win one more board game ("bored games," we call them between ourselves), and sometimes we wistfully talk about the days before we had children—days when sleeping in was a possibility, no one needed us to wipe their bottom, and we ate actual grown-up food instead of rotating between chicken nuggets and fish sticks.

We aren't perfect parents by far, but even we have seen the ill effects clutter can have on kids. Not just physical clutter—massive piles of plastic junk—but schedule clutter and digital clutter and soul clutter, too. The effects of such mess is bad enough on adults; on our kids it is magnified. Kids are *kids*—they lack advanced decision-making skills, processing abilities, and the capacity to handle highly complex tasks. But kids' brains begin learning and forming habits early. If their environments and schedules are cluttered; if they are given hours of screen time and no Sabbath; if they are trained to hoard and cling; these patterns can create unhealthy habits that will affect the rest of their lives.

> IF KIDS ARE TRAINED TO HOARD AND CLING, THESE PATTERNS CAN CREATE UNHEALTHY HABITS THAT WILL AFFECT THE REST OF THEIR LIVES.

Not only that, but as I've continued to learn firsthand how hard it is to break the habits of clutter, I've wanted more than anything a fresh path for our kids.

A different path. One unmarked by the sins of my adulthood, the stockpiling of stuff and the cramming-in of activities and the hours that add up to days given up to the vast abyss of social media.

If it's hard for those of us who first met the digital age as teenagers or adults to keep technology in its proper place, how can we expect our kids to have even a fighting chance without help? For all these reasons, in our house we seek to cultivate a simple childhood for our littles: one majoring in creativity, generosity, imagination, and joy.

One of the things we've found most helpful in teaching habits of godly simplicity to our kids is reciting homemade proverbs. Easily repeatable maxims of faithfulness that our kids are memorizing alongside us. Daryl and I wrote and adopted these seven to help guard a simple childhood for our kiddos. Perhaps they may help you, too.

1. God first.

When kids came along, living God-first became even trickier. It's amazing how often our culture puts forth idols that look so good it seems they couldn't *possibly* be idols. Nearly every Christian would agree that excessive wealth can be an idol, but our children? How could we *not* put them first?

There were parts of raising our kids to know Jesus that were straightforward. We attend communal worship each Sunday; we read a children's Bible with them before bed; we're teaching them to pray. But when it came to concrete family decisions about stuff and schedule, things felt more confusing. What if soccer practice got switched to Sunday mornings? How many pieces of PJ Masks memorabilia was it healthy and reasonable for our Catboy-obsessed son to own? What if our youngest really *would* be developmentally behind unless we scraped together enough money to get him into the Mommy & Me class at the local community college? (This wasn't suggested by our pediatrician, but by another mom on the playground.) God first, of course, but didn't he want us to put our children first?

Nope. Look at Jesus' strong words in Matthew's gospel: "Anyone who loves their father or mother more than me is not worthy of me; anyone who loves their son or daughter more than me is not worthy of me."[82] The family, properly ordered, puts God first. Every other decision about our children flows from this singular priority.

It turns out this is not just a biblical decision; it's a practical one as well. Dr. Michael Mascolo writes of the problems of parenting styles that are child-first, "Child-centered parenting runs the risk of producing entitled, narcissistic children who lack the capacity to persevere and cope with difficulty."[83] A loving Christian family raises children lovingly—cultivating boundaries straight from God's heart. We are to have no other gods before the Lord, not even the tiny tykes who so early steal our hearts. The family should not revolve around the children; not only because God asks us to order our homes under his Lordship, but because a child-centered family isn't healthy for the kids, either.

One pastor puts it this way: "How can we expect our kids to know the true God when we teach them that *they* are God?" Ouch. And also, amen.

Do the kids want to play baseball on a Sunday morning? The question becomes not, "Do they want to?" or "Is it fun for them?" or even "Will this affect their baseball prospects in the years ahead?" but "What would God have us do?" If God is really serious about the commands to keep the Sabbath holy, to have no idols, and to worship the Lord and serve him only, the decision becomes clearer. Not easier, perhaps, but clearer. One family with whom we are close found a Saturday

> THE FAMILY, PROPERLY ORDERED, PUTS GOD FIRST. EVERY OTHER DECISION ABOUT OUR CHILDREN FLOWS FROM THIS SINGULAR PRIORITY.

night worship service so their son could keep up with his sport. Another helped invest in a new sport for their daughter, since their church's services conflicted with her games. It was gut-wrenching, but they wanted to teach her from a young age that God comes first. Decisions like this speak much more loudly than words to both our children and our community.

We can trust God with the good of our children. He loves them even more than we do. He knows our children on an even more intimate level than we do—he created them! When we put God above all else, allowing him to order our schedules, our stuff, and our souls, we put ourselves in the very best hands possible.

2. We believe God's heart is one of openness and joy.

How do you eliminate clutter—both physical and logistical—without becoming the Grinch that stole Christmas? Minimalists, and those who find themselves living a lifestyle that's minimalist-ish, are notorious curmudgeons when it comes to receiving gifts.

"Oh *goody*," they say, rolling their eyes, "more Legos." "What is this plastic abomination?" they shriek with horror. "We only let our kids play with locally sourced organic natural wood toys!" While minimalism is often aesthetically driven, Christian simplicity centers on virtue, openness, and joy. Beauty is important; so is sustainability. But they don't trump kindness or mercy or grace, receiving from others with gratitude and thankfulness.

Not to mention the fact that you get more flies with honey, as the saying goes, and kids are more likely to feel an affinity for a faith of generosity and joy than one of stinginess and crankitude. Jesus himself was incredibly joyful, flexible, and kind. "Let the little children come to me," Jesus tells his disciples as they try to shield him from a small mob of sticky-faced kidlets. "Do not hinder them," he continues, "for the kingdom of heaven belongs to such as these."[84] What we've found is that uncluttering allows more space in our home for play and creativity and fellowship and fun. If it makes us rigid and uncaring in the possessions we invite and the activities we allow, then we've missed the spirit of God's invitation to us.

As a child, I attended Sunday school with a family of six kids whose parents decided that receiving gifts went against the biblical meaning of Christmas. There's certainly an argument to be made there, especially in light of our increasingly consumer-driven culture. So this family simply opted out of Christmas gifts. As an adult seeking an uncluttered life, I respect this tremendously. As a kid, I remember thinking, "If that's what it means to be a Christian, then I *refuse to be one.*" While each family needs to prayerfully make its own decisions (and this family's kids all grew up to love Jesus, so clearly it worked for them!), we have chosen to celebrate kid birthdays in our house with small, modest parties and a few gifts. At Christmastime the grandparents give our sons Nerf blasters and baseball mitts and colored pencil sets and yes, those dreaded loud and flashy plastic toys that we pray lose battery power ASAP. These things add to the clutter, and for that reason they won't all remain forever. But they also bring joy, reminding us that celebration is a spiritual practice, too.

We work hard to curtail clutter, but we also strive to understand what it is to be a kid in an uncluttered household, growing to love Jesus and to understand the virtue of Christian simplicity. If we teach our children the values of an uncluttered life 362 days of the year, letting loose on the other three won't kill anyone. In fact, it may save them.

3. We will seek to foster generosity.

"You know, Mommy," Lincoln, then four years old, told me early one morning, twirling a pair of my glasses between his fingers, "you have *two* pairs of glasses, which is more than you need. If you have more than you need of something, you should give it away to someone who doesn't have any. Like me. I don't have any glasses." He put them crookedly on his little face and ran off down the hallway.

Daryl started chuckling. "How are you going to explain to him that you need at least two pairs of glasses because you're always losing one?" he asked. "But at least he's learning something about generosity."

One of the reasons we seek an uncluttered life is so that we have enough room left to bless others. When Lincoln was still a toddler, we began this conversation with him. One afternoon he noticed a boy in our neighborhood who didn't have as many toys and mentioned it to us.

"How many toys do you have?" Daryl asked.

"A *lot*," said Lincoln. Then he paused. "But I need them all."

We pulled out his bin of cars—all eighty-four thousand of them—and asked if there were a few he might want to give away to his new friend. He bit his lip. His eyes welled with tears.

"How about this?" I asked. "You don't have to give away any of your cars if you don't want to. But if you *did* want to, for each car you put in this grocery bag here," I went to the kitchen and came back with the bag and a box of jelly beans, "you could have a jelly bean." He lit up. Lincoln would sell me, his own mother, up the river for a jelly bean.

"I probably don't need *all* my cars," he said. For the next ten minutes we went through his bin. He discovered duplicates of a couple of cars, set his favorites back on his shelf, and put twenty-seven cars into the grocery bag all on his own. Turned out we had one generous and now completely sugared-up child. I texted our neighbor, and she invited us over. We rang her bell, and she answered the door with her son.

> GENEROSITY IS LEARNED, AND WE ARE ON THE FRONT LINES OF INSTRUCTION.

"These are cars I like," Lincoln said, holding out the grocery bag to the toddler, "but I like you too. Do you want some cars?" The boy grinned and immediately held his arms out, reaching first not for the bag of cars, but for a hug.

Generosity doesn't come naturally to most of us, but the earlier we begin to foster it in our kids, the sooner it will become part of their stock of habits. Generosity is learned, and we are on the front lines of instruction. This was one thing my mom and dad sought to nurture in my sisters and me growing up. I didn't always like it then, but looking back I see the wisdom in their instruction.

One particular example stands out. My family celebrated each week's end with a Friday pizza-and-movie night. It was part of our family liturgy, and we all looked forward to it. My sisters and I secretly loved our weekly tiffs over which title to rent from the green-roofed Primetime Video store, which pizza toppings we'd beg my parents to order from Pizza Hut, and whether we could persuade them to let us drink soda *just this once* (an argument we repeated weekly without ever noticing the irony). Then one week, on the snowy drive to the video rental place, my mom broke some surprising news.

"We aren't renting a video this week," she said. My sisters and I raised immediate alarm. "I'm not finished," she said. "We aren't renting a video because we are going to do something else instead." She and my dad explained that the cost of our weekly pizza-and-movie family night ran about thirty dollars. "There are a lot of hungry people in this town. How many groceries do you think we could buy with that same amount of money?" she asked.

She and my dad drove our minivan to the supermarket where we walked down the aisles as a family picking out food pantry staples—pasta and peanut butter and canned goods. Turns out we could buy a *lot* of groceries for the same amount of money we spent on a pizza or two and a PG-rated '90s film. How many times could we really watch *Home Alone II: Lost in*

New York anyway? We dropped the goods off at the local pantry and went home to eat leftovers and play Monopoly. I missed watching a movie; I won't say I didn't. But the silence and space in a Friday evening without our usual video distraction spoke volumes. My parents never brought it up again. My sisters and I never forgot it. (Except for Caroline. But her memory's terrible.)

4. In our home, Jesus will be given more airtime than any cartoon, mythical figure, or pop icon.

Kids love a good story. I'm guessing you, like me, have your own childhood favorites. I was a My-Little-Pony-obsessed kid, and I can still recite some of their television episodes from memory. We only got a few fuzzy channels in the Wisconsin woods, so my grandmother would tape episodes for me at her house in Chicago and bring them up when she came to visit. I watched those VHS tapes until they wore out, but don't worry, the flutter ponies *did* save Flutter Valley from the evil Queen Bumble. My husband could tell you every single thing Knight Rider can do. Stories are great. Television is not inherently evil, but, like all things, it needs proper ordering, or it turns into a Master Clutterer.

Giving Jesus more airtime than cartoons or myths or pop culture doesn't mean we only read the Bible and listen to Christian radio. It means we give more time to things that honor God and nurture virtue than things that are neutral or secular. Working with our hands honors God; loving our neighbors does as well. We speak of Jesus within the walls of our home as a more real, important, valuable, and loving figure than any other because, you know, he *is*. The amount of time we give to something speaks volumes about what is most important to us. What do we want our kids to hear?

5. Whenever possible, we will create rather than consume.

When life gets stressful, I bake. While we attended seminary, Daryl would often come home to kitchen counters covered with muffins and brownies and loaves and pies. By then we'd been married for a couple of years, so he knew exactly what to ask.

"Are you okay?"

Baking relieves anxiety for me because after I bake, I have successfully created something. I don't always eat everything I bake (if I did, my doctor would have THINGS to say to me; I bake a *lot*). It isn't the sugar rush that calms me; it's the act of creation. After sitting in a long committee meeting where nothing seems to get accomplished, hashing out a difficult transition with the kids that didn't go particularly well, or folding yet another load of clothes in our never-ending heap of laundry, sometimes I have to make something with my hands that turns into a finished product in front of my eyes. Even when the world is burning, if you put eggs and sugar and peanut butter in a bowl, mix it up, and bake it, you get cookies. Shalom.

We were created to create. To make things and build things and paint things and cook things. Yet we live in a culture of consumerism where purchasing and squandering, depleting and expending are far more common than creating. Choosing to create takes intentionality and planning, but oh, the results are so satisfying and real and good!

Beyond that, creating is active, while consuming is passive. As first and ultimate Creator, God shaped the world into being and sustains his good creation. When we create, we participate in this faithful work and connect with ourselves, our communities, and our God in deeper and more profound ways.

It isn't that consuming is inherently bad. Who among us doesn't enjoy a dinner cooked by someone else (and perhaps even more, *dishes* washed by someone else)? Who in our midst lives in a house they built with their own hands, wired by gadgets they put together from loose parts? Sometimes consumption is necessary. Sometimes it's *good*. But it too easily becomes our default, and then we become consumers first and creators (and perhaps even Christians) a far, far second.

Andy Crouch recommends making music rather than playing it, teaching our children what it is to raise their voices in praise to God rather than exclusively rocking out to the latest pop hits or Disneyfied theme song. He writes, "To sing . . . is to know wisdom. And it's also to develop the courage and character to declare that God is this good, and we are this in need of him, that we are this thankful, that we are this committed to be part of his story."[85] Singing isn't about performance-level music-making, it's about willingness and love and heart.

> WHEN WE CREATE, WE PARTICIPATE IN THIS FAITHFUL WORK AND CONNECT WITH OURSELVES, OUR COMMUNITIES, AND OUR GOD IN DEEPER AND MORE PROFOUND WAYS.

I have a musical background; Daryl does not. I grew up singing in church, practicing eight thousand hours of piano, playing guitar in the youth group (cool!) and the French horn in the school band (so not cool!). I grew up creating music; he grew up consuming it. For that reason, he's always been a bit self-conscious about his singing. It isn't that he can't sing; it's that he never learned the basics of reading music. Yet after finishing Crouch's chapter on "Why Singing Matters," he was convinced. Daryl printed up a few pages of hymn lyrics, posted them in the kitchen, and started creating music of his own.

"What are you doing?" Lincoln asked, raising a sarcastic eyebrow.

"Singing praise to Jesus," said Daryl. Linc pondered this, went back to his train set, and before long, lifted his voice alongside his daddy in praise.

We create in a myriad of different ways, from building to baking, gardening to music-making, writing to painting. Kids are wired to love creating—most of them haven't yet learned our culture's derision for handcrafted gifts and less-than-perfect artwork. As we expose them to things we are creating and give them opportunities to build and experiment and make and do, they will begin to lose themselves in the sacred act of creation—one of the most holy acts a human being can participate in.

To help facilitate this for our kids and their friends, we've set up stations around the house with art supplies, spaces in the garage with hammers and nails and scrap wood, outdoor areas where they can "garden." (My toddler, Wilson, does this by digging up plants and smashing them on top of other plants.

It's his favorite hobby, and I've had to make peace with the reality that, for a toddler, creating often looks a lot like destroying.)

There's no end to what kids can create, and there's meaning even in their messes. Make wrapping paper, birthday cards, letters for Grandma. Let them help out when you make dinner or breakfast or dessert. Whenever possible, ask, "Could we make this instead of purchasing it?" Creativity breeds creativity, so don't be surprised when, after a rocky start, it starts to get easier and more fun. We grow kale and broccoli and Swiss chard in the backyard now, and both kids actually *eat them* because they've helped plant and harvest. Small organic miracles are no less miraculous.

6. We will allow our kids to be bored.

Since when did boredom become the enemy? If I complained to my parents I felt bored, they'd give me a chore to do. Guess how long it took me to stop complaining? Yes, kids who are bored can get themselves into trouble. But they can also find rhythms of rest and creativity and imagination. If we never allow our children to be bored, we fail to provide them with opportunities to listen to the quiet voice inside them telling them who they are and what they need. Inevitably, when Lincoln is bored, he spends about ten minutes kvetching. If we wait out those ten minutes, he'll disappear into the backyard or his bedroom and discover something interesting on his own. Sometimes it's building a fort or riding his bike; other times it's snuggling up with a blanket and a book. Occasionally we have to give him ideas: "Puzzle? Soccer ball? Legos?" or pull down a bin of toys, but if we wait, he usually finds his way on his own. Regardless, in pushing through those ten minutes of fidgety frustration, both he and his parents discover that not all discomfort needs to be immediately quelled. If we run to him with screens the moment he's fidgety, what will he learn?

Part of uncluttering our kids is allowing them to learn about themselves—who they are, what they enjoy, how to feel psychological discomfort without collapsing into themselves like a dying star. Learning about ourselves takes time and space and quiet. It takes long, slow afternoons filled with nothing busy or flashy or loud. My friend Ginger posted a picture of her son, Edward, on Facebook a while back. He proudly held a stick with a caterpillar curled around it up to the camera, grinning like he'd won a trophy. Above it she wrote:

> We have consciously chosen not to enroll our children in after school programs or the current season's sport. This may seem odd to many, but our lives entirely consist of family, church,

school, and medical appointments. Why? Because when Edward finds a caterpillar on an Indian summer evening, we want to give him the space to play with his new furry pet until the sun goes down. We've chosen to define our own moments.[86]

For Ginger and her young sons, church and family and school took up enough time without adding other extracurriculars. The kids needed time to play rather than be rushed from activity to activity. We've chosen something similar.

"But wait!" you might be saying. "Kids need to be well-rounded!" Well, yes and no. And we haven't eschewed all activities like Ginger and her brood, though we only do very few. When our firstborn was tiny, I went to a music class with him. Forty-five minutes each week of singing and bouncing and clapping. It fit within his nap schedule, and it was life-giving for us both. When he was four, we put him in ten weeks of summer swim lessons. Now that he's five, he plays soccer for forty-five minutes each week with his buddies. His little brother has taken his place in the music class.

Kids need things to do, it's true. My middle sister has four kids and lives in north-north-*north* Minnesota. In the winter it gets dark at 3:30 p.m., and it's too cold to go outside for more than a few minutes at a time. If it wasn't for ice hockey, her kids might gnaw their own arms off out of boredom. So they play hockey. A *lot* of hockey. But they don't also do ballet, chess club, gymnastics, Awana, and Girl Scouts. When it comes to kid activities, balance is key. Just because all the other parents are all in on the water ballet league five nights a week doesn't mean you have to be, too.

7. Until our kids are in high school, screens will be saved for special occasions.

This may sound draconian, but it's been one of our most life-giving and uncluttering parenting decisions by far. Do you know who else kept digital screens away from their kids? Mega tech giants. In 2007, Gates' then ten-year-old daughter didn't start using a computer regularly until it was required for school. After that she had a forty-five minute limit each day.[87] A *New York Times* reporter asked Steve Jobs in 2014 whether his kids loved Apple's newest gadget, the iPad.

"They haven't used it," he replied. "We limit how much technology our kids use at home."[88] Sean Parker, former president of Facebook, admitted that his platform was designed to "consume as much of your time and conscious attention as possible." Noted Parker,

"God only knows what it's doing to our children's brains."[89]

Six days a week our five-year-old watches no television, plays on no smartphones, and sees no tablets. On our family Sabbath, he gets to watch a preapproved movie or a few episodes of an appropriate show. That's the family plan for about forty-nine weeks out of the year. Other than that: no screens.

Of course, there are exceptions to this. Just this week Daryl and I were so knock-down, flat-out exhausted from sleep battles we've been having with the toddler and illnesses of our own that we napped on a Saturday morning while the five-year-old watched a few episodes of *The Magic School Bus.* On airplanes we mainline any type of digital media that will keep the kids in their seats and reasonably quiet. If UCLA makes it to the Elite Eight in March, all television boundaries fail to exist. Isolated examples do occur, and after they do there's often a period of whining as the kids detox. But by and large we stick to our guns: no special occasion, no screens.

These are the seven principles we've adopted to help give the children God has entrusted to us an uncluttered childhood. At times each requires a sacrifice of us, their parents. Screens are ubiquitous; consuming is far easier than creating; and following the cult of kid-centrism is much simpler than following Jesus in twenty-first-century America. And yet, I wouldn't trade our little life for all the ease in the world. After all, anything worth doing takes some sacrifice, and raising kids is one of the best, hardest, most important things we will ever do. It might even be *the* most important.

And that's coming from a decidedly non-kid-centric parent.

Generosity

FREE THE FINANCES

*If a person gets his attitude toward money
straight, it will help straighten out almost
every other area in his life.*
–Billy Graham

Kent Hughes, longtime pastor at College Church in
Wheaton, tells the story of a pastor who visited a
rural farmer.

"If you had $200, would you give $100 to the Lord?"
asked the pastor.

"Sure would," said the farmer.

"If you had two cows, would you give God one?"
asked the pastor.

"I think so, yes," said the farmer.

"If you had two pigs, would you give one to God?" asked the pastor.

"Well now, that's not fair," said the farmer. "You *know* I have two pigs."[90]

One of the hardest lessons I've had to learn is that my money belongs to God. Every dollar. Every cent. Every credit card. Every check. No matter whose face they put on the new ten dollar bill, that belongs to God, too. Sometimes it's actually easier to acknowledge that our lives are God's and that our bodies are God's than to acknowledge that our money is God's. Because...yikes. God is a little bit unhinged when it comes to generosity and courage and teaching us to trust, isn't he? Jesus tells us that the last will be first, that it is easier for a camel to go through the eye of the needle than for a rich person to go into heaven, that the kingdom of heaven is like a mustard seed. How can you trust someone like that with your money? Doesn't he understand cost of living? When it starts to get personal, it can make us want to run. Want to sit on our wallets and our hands, just in case we're tempted to do something silly, like let God handle our finances.

Giving is most difficult when it's personal. When it's our money, our time, our talent, our pigs. God knows this. Of course he knows. Not a sparrow can fall to the ground without his notice. Not a dollar can be earned that he does not see. God wants us to open our lives to him fully—financially—because he wants to set us free. Freedom does not come from having control of our lives. It doesn't come from finally earning enough that we are comfortable, that we have a little bit extra, that we don't have to trust God at all. Freedom comes in submitting to the Lordship of the one who created us, who sent his son Jesus Christ to live and die and rise again for us—for you—so that we could live. Not in financial greed or financial fear or financial anxiety, but in the freedom of knowing that God cares for the lilies of the field and the birds of the air, and God will provide for us, too. Whether you have a lot or a little—all you have is the Lord's, and he will provide.

> GOD WANTS US TO OPEN OUR LIVES TO HIM FULLY—FINANCIALLY—BECAUSE HE WANTS TO SET US FREE.

One of the truths that's kept me tethered to Jesus when life gets stormy is that he always goes first. Even when it comes to money, Jesus is not asking anything of us that he has not done first himself. Second Corinthians 8:9 reads, "For you know the grace of our Lord Jesus Christ, that though he was rich, yet for your sake he became poor, so that you through his poverty might become rich." Jesus came down from heaven to live among us. From the glory of his Father's presence to a tumbledown stable. From the heights of heaven to the pain and suffering of a human body. Jesus has lived a life of utter openness to God so that we can do the same, following in his footsteps, emptying our lives of all but him.

The Grace of the Tithe

Decades ago, when my sisters and I sold homemade crafts at an annual festival in our tiny Wisconsin hometown (population 1,304), my mom would help us count out our earnings into four piles at the end of the day.

"This is to pay me back for the supplies," she'd say, pointing to the first pile. "This is for your savings," the second one. "This is for church," the third. "And this is for you," the fourth and final pile. We'd all look down in dismay. How'd we end up with such a small cut of our own hard-earned cash? How many gummy bears and Baby-sitters Club novels could twenty-five dollars even *buy*? We knew we couldn't talk her out of getting her supply money back, or the percentage that

> JESUS HAS LIVED A LIFE OF UTTER OPENNESS TO GOD SO THAT WE CAN DO THE SAME, FOLLOWING IN HIS FOOTSTEPS, EMPTYING OUR LIVES OF ALL BUT HIM.

was earmarked for our savings accounts, but we looked hungrily at the tithing pile.

"We give 10 percent to church," Mom said. "Always. Every time."

Her lesson stuck with me, and I'm glad it began early because setting aside a percentage of my income for Jesus has only gotten harder as I've grown. It's one thing giving five dollars out of fifty to Jesus. It was a whole different ball game giving fifty dollars out of five hundred in graduate school, especially when that five hundred was all I had for gas, groceries, and household supplies for the next month. Make that four hundred and fifty. Thanks, *Jesus*.

It's harder still today, when that 10 percent could go into my children's college funds or pay for new carpet that we desperately need (our current flooring makes me sneeze like one of the seven dwarves ...). The more we have, the harder it is to give such a big percentage to God, because the more we have, the bigger that percentage seems. A dollar out of ten? No problem. A hundred thousand dollars out of a million (not that this is my current dilemma, but there's always the off chance I'll be invited to compete on Wheel of Fortune!)? That sounds crazy-go-nuts. What does Jesus want with our cash, anyway? Doesn't he own, like, the whole universe?

Turns out tithing isn't for God. As the psalmist reminds us, he owns "the cattle on a thousand hills."[91] He doesn't need our dollar bills; what he needs is our hearts. And all too often our hearts are more entangled with our wallets and our bank accounts and our financial problems than they are with the living Jesus Christ. So God gives us the grace of asking for some of it back so we can learn what it is to be generous, to be open, to be free. Because when our finances are cluttered by worry rather than opened in trust, we live in bondage. Fearfully clinging to what we have is no way to live. As Brené Brown notes in *Daring Greatly*, "The counterapproach to living in scarcity isn't abundance. The opposite of scarcity is *enough*."[92]

My uncle Del is a musician, and one of his songs sticks in my mind in seasons when I'm worried there won't be enough. The chorus goes:

> All that I've needed
> He has provided
> He already knew[93]

God *already* knew. The God who clothes the lilies and feeds the sparrows loves us and knows our needs. Not just our wants—which God often allows to go unfulfilled for the sake of our souls—but our needs, our legitimate physical and emotional and spiritual and social needs. God knows them. And if we trust in him, those needs will get met without us striving and grasping and insisting on how it will all get done.

Where Your Treasure Is…

The Bible minces no words on money, because money can insulate us from God and from our neighbors. It must be faced head-on and discussed without flinching. The first step for Daryl and me in uncluttering our finances was to make a commitment to tithe, giving the first 10 percent of our income to Jesus with absolutely no strings attached.

This was easier for me than for Daryl, in part because he keeps the family's finances and budget. Numbers aren't really my thing. The idea of tithing sounded good to me. I'd done it as a kid and been faithful in it, for the most part, through my teenage years and into young adulthood. It seemed like a given: if not a scriptural command, then at least a strong, for-our-own-good suggestion. I felt more than a little bit holier than my husband, who wasn't totally sold on the practice. Wasn't he lucky to have me, the one

ALL TOO OFTEN OUR HEARTS ARE MORE ENTANGLED WITH OUR WALLETS AND OUR BANK ACCOUNTS AND OUR FINANCIAL PROBLEMS THAN THEY ARE WITH THE LIVING JESUS CHRIST.

who wanted to obey Jesus no matter the cost? I was all high and mighty and proud of myself until Daryl showed me the family budget.

"Whoa," I said, looking at the spreadsheet he'd crafted with our fixed expenses, flexible expenses, and income. "That 10 percent makes a *huge* difference. If we could just keep *some of it...*" He looked me straight in the eye.

"Do *not* go there," he said. "If we're going to do this, we're going to have to stop thinking like that and start trusting that God really will provide." Turns out it takes two to tithe, at least when one manages the budget and the other has the math skills of a cross-eyed raccoon. (I majored in literature for a reason.)

The challenge of tithing isn't unique to you and me, though. Tithing has always been hard. No matter how much or how little money we make, our "necessary" expenses tend to grow with our income. As multi-millionaire J. D. Rockefeller is said to have quipped, "How much money is enough? Just a little bit more."[94] Back in biblical times, people often held back their best from God, hoping he wouldn't notice. Cain brought God some produce from his garden, but not the best. In Malachi the prophet laments the sins of the nation, bringing them the message of an angry God:

"You ask, 'How are we robbing you?'

"In tithes and offerings. You are under a curse—your whole nation—because you are robbing me. Bring the *whole* tithe into the storehouse."[95] In Acts 5, Ananias and Sapphira find themselves meeting their Maker before their time when they try to keep back money from God. It is human nature to strive and grasp and cling to each dollar. But clinging is the opposite of freedom, and God created us to live in freedom, our hands open to receive his gifts and praise him in unencumbered worship.

> THE BEGINNING OF AN UNCLUTTERED FINANCIAL LIFE IS REALIZING EVERYTHING WE HAVE COMES FROM GOD.

It turns out that tithing is a vital key to uncluttering our finances, and having simple finances is an even more critical step to uncluttering our souls.

Where to Begin?

The beginning of an uncluttered financial life is realizing everything we have comes from God. Everything. Not just our possessions, but our vocations, our families, our homes, our vehicles, our jobs, our bodies, our souls, our very lives. Paul puts it this way in the book of Colossians: "For in him all things were created: things in heaven and on earth, visible and invisible, whether thrones or powers or rulers or authorities; all things have been created through him and for him."[96] Daryl, who tends to be straight-to-the-point, once framed it like this: "God could ask absolutely everything of us. We owe him our very lives. So really, 10 percent is a pretty good deal."

We began tithing fairly early in our marriage. In my first pastorate we lived in a manse—the church-owned parsonage—rent-free. Tithing there was pretty easy. Sure, there were a few bigger purchases we had to save for that we otherwise could have purchased sooner, but we weren't in any danger of going hungry or homeless. Then God called us out to southern California where our cost of living quadrupled. (That's not an exaggeration. I literally had to pretend we were spending Monopoly money for the first few months to avoid having panic attacks. I had no earthly idea how we were going to survive financially.) For the first time since I was in graduate school, tithing became not just a small sacrifice but a painful one. There were things we couldn't do, places we couldn't go, food we couldn't buy because of our tithe.

(A brief note here: there may be seasons when it's literally impossible for you to give 10 percent of your income to God. *That is okay.* In seminary, Daryl and I went through a season of very little income and staggering dental bills because apparently most people's teeth are made of enamel but mine are made out of papier-mâché. We paid those dental bills and the rent and the health insurance and the grocery bill and we didn't tithe. We couldn't tithe. God understood. But we must not confuse what feels impossible with what

> OPEN YOUR FINANCIAL LIFE UP TO JESUS, LETTING HIS PRIORITIES BECOME YOUR OWN.

simply feels good because it leaves us with more money in our pockets and complete control of our finances. When we began our first jobs out of seminary and paid off those dental bills, we began tithing again. It was incredibly tempting not to. Hoarding habits run deep, friends, and there was a lot we wanted to do with those dollars, but with God's grace we stuck to our guns.)

If you've never ordered your finances in this way, it will take some getting used to. Perhaps you can give 1 percent this month and 2 percent the next, until you reach 10 percent. If you're married and your spouse isn't on board, the tithe may need to come from your personal income or your portion of the spending money. That's okay, too. The key is to open your financial life up to Jesus, letting his priorities become your own.

It's Not about the Money, Money, Money

As Jessie J. sings, it's *not* about the money. It actually isn't, at least not at the root. Tithing is about deciding which of the following two things we allow to reign in our hearts and our families: trust or worry. Do we trust that God is who he says he is? That he has our best interests at heart? That he will provide for our needs? Or will we let worry—a mind-set of scarcity and fear—run the show? Fear breeds fear. Worry compounds worry. But trust? It paves the way for peace and freedom and joy and hope. And this is where God loves to break through.

TRUST PAVES THE WAY FOR PEACE AND FREEDOM AND JOY AND HOPE.

Our first months in California, we quickly realized we needed to be frugal-beyond-frugal, and we learned to watch every penny. The tithe remained, but boy, did we notice it every month. And in noticing it, we noticed our needs, which in turn opened our eyes anew to the ways God met them—each and every single time—in surprising and humbling and completely beautiful ways.

Tithing pushed us (and continues to push us) to greater, deeper, simpler faith. It properly ordered our finances under the God who created us, loves us, and knows our need. And in the grand scheme of uncluttering, having less money to spend on us and more to give to Jesus has meant a freer space and a lighter soul. What's in my wallet these days? Not quite as much. And, believe it or not, I'm glad.

Worship

THE ULTIMATE UNCLUTTERED ACT

Once you begin, you should never again
resemble the people you once were.

–Brenda Salter McNeil

After our second-born arrived, my midwife gave it to me straight. "Your core strength is gone," she said. "You'll need to slowly build it back up for the sake of your back, your posture, and your overall health. It's all about the core." Our youngest is two now, and my core is still a little wobbly. Who has time for core work? I had things to do, people to see, brownies to eat.

Then an ankle injury sent me to physical therapy, where a kind but no-nonsense PT looked me over and said, "That core needs work, too."

"I'm here for a sprained ankle..." I protested weakly.

"Doesn't matter," she said. "No core strength, no strength."

By now we've covered over a dozen angles on the Christian virtue of simplicity, from homes to schedules to finances to the digital space. An uncluttered home is a beautiful thing. An uncluttered schedule brings freedom. An uncluttered digital life invites peace into our souls. But really, without a strong core, we can only grow so much. It's time to talk about the ultimate uncluttered act: worship.

For all the hard work we put in reducing our possessions and shaving down our schedules, practicing hospitality and hopping off the busyness train, our lives will remain cluttered without regular, repeated, continual worship of the living God. This begins in communal worship, when we gather with our fellow sinners and saints in the church to praise and pray and hear the ancient words of Scripture proclaimed once again as true and radical and beautiful and right. Though this communal act is absolutely essential, worship goes beyond the Sunday hour. Communal worship as part of a Christ-centered congregation is a beginning, not an end—an invitation into the life of worship we were created for.

In *The Dangerous Act of Worship*, Mark Labberton describes this type of worship: "The core of a biblical theology of worship is the worthiness of God," he writes. "Worship is about this God and for this God."[97] The paradox of uncluttering is that we begin to learn to find this majestic, magnificent, all-powerful God in the small, immediate, ordinary things of life. When we have less, God becomes more. When we do less, God looms ever larger. And the way we keep going back to the well of this living water—the presence that refreshes us for the journey, orders our lives in love, and supplies our every need—is in the act of worship.

Only in worship are we simplified down to our most basic identity—people created in and through Jesus Christ to worship our creator—Father, Son, and Holy Spirit. As the ancient Westminster Confession puts it, "The chief end of [humanity] is to glorify God and enjoy him forever."[98] This is our purpose, our goal, our ultimate reason for existing. Worship puts this glorification front and center, orienting the rest of our lives, our vocations, our possessions, our schedules, our souls aright and anew.

COMMUNAL WORSHIP AS PART OF A CHRIST-CENTERED CONGREGATION IS A BEGINNING, NOT AN END – AN INVITATION INTO THE LIFE OF WORSHIP WE WERE CREATED FOR.

It is easy, of course, to make worship about us. It's the human condition—we're narcissists, all of us, when it gets right down to it. We all too quickly begin to think about Sunday mornings in terms of "what I get out of it" and "did that sermon speak to me" and "how do I feel about that electric guitar?" It isn't that biblical integrity doesn't matter—of course it does. But worship that becomes about our musical preference or desired preaching style or even scheduling convenience rather than responding to God with the honor due his name—this is a dangerous game indeed. Notes Labberton, "We need worship to clarify the danger. We need to meet God in order to know what's worth fearing and what's not."[99]

What, then, is worth fearing? It's not a popular sentiment in an age where we've learned to embrace Jesus as our buddy, our brother, our friend, but the truth is that much of what lies diseased and disordered in our culture and in our lives comes from fearing the wrong things and failing to fear the right one. We store up possessions because we fear not having enough. We overschedule because we fear not being enough. We stay busy because we fear what we may face within ourselves if we are ever still or silent. We fear what we should not and fail to fear what we must.

William Barclay tells the story of Hugh Latimer, a Christian bishop in England in the 1500s. Latimer was preaching when King Henry VIII was present. He knew that he was about to say something that would anger the king, and in those days, that could easily get a person killed. So in the pulpit he began speaking to himself, saying: "Latimer! Latimer! Latimer! Be careful what you say. Henry the king is here." Then he paused for a moment, prayerfully.

"Latimer! Latimer! Latimer!" he continued. "Be careful what you say. *The King of Kings is here.*"[100] Latimer knew who his most important audience was: God, the creator of the heavens and the earth. He had a holy fear, a holy respect for God. Latimer didn't lose his life that day, but later, at the hands of another English monarch. Yet in losing his life, he gained eternity.

This is what we have found as we sought to follow Jesus in uncluttering every area of our lives. For all we have given up, we have gained far more, and what we have gained is eternal. In instances when we are tempted to hoard, to store up, to seek to control, we've often thought of the wise words of Jim Elliot: "He is no fool to give what he cannot keep to gain that which he cannot lose."[101]

Bonhoeffer echoed this searing insight in a sermon he wrote in 1935 called "Learning to Die." He wrote:

> Fear God—instead of the many things which you fear. Do not fear the coming day, do not

fear other people, do not fear power and might, even if they are able to deprive you of property and life; do not fear the great ones of this world; do not even fear yourselves; do not fear sin. All this fear will be the death of you. You are free from all this fear; it isn't there for you. But fear God and God alone; for God has power over the powers of this world; the whole world must fear God—God has power to give us life or to destroy us; everything else is a game—only God is in earnest, entirely in earnest. Fear God's earnestness—and give God the glory.[102]

The heart of an uncluttered life is the glory of the God who created us, loves us, sustains us, and calls us forth.

Made to Worship

While regular weekly worship is essential, where an uncluttered heart learns to beat in rhythm with its creator, worship will never be limited to a Sunday morning. It overflows into all of life, soaking us to the skin with the living water of Jesus. God doesn't ask us for a piece of our weeks; he asks us for our heart, our soul, our mind, and our strength. As Carlo Carretto writes in *The God Who Comes*, "By his choice, his relationship with me is a presence, as a call, as a guide; he is not satisfied with speaking to me, or showing things to me, or asking things of me. He does much more."[103]

As we draw closer to Jesus in weekly worship, we will be invited and formed into the type of person who worships him with every other area and every other hour of our lives. Worship opens up the space for God to unclutter our hearts and lives. Without worship, we will remain blind to our clutter. In God's presence, however, we gradually see ourselves as we truly are and as God wants to make us. As the psalmist writes, "In your light we see light."[104]

Worship allows God to loosen our hold on our possessions, helping us to see them as they truly are— objects we can use to bless our neighbors or raise our kids or create new works of art—means to ends and not ends in and of themselves. Worship allows God to push us into greater hospitality, giving us Jesus' heart for the stranger, the alien, the newcomer, the one waiting on the margins for an invitation to the feast. Worship allows God to anchor us to what is real—creation, neighbor, stranger, friend—and helps us keep digital ephemera in its proper place. Worship will sing to us the unending song of God's provision, helping us open our finances to the Lord of life.

There's a reason the book of Revelation paints a picture of the new heaven and the new earth as places of worship above all else. Worship is our end; it's what we are made for . . . it's the uncluttered climax toward which the whole world is headed. Henri Nouwen describes it this way:

> To walk in the presence of the Lord means to move forward in life in such a way that all our desires, thoughts, and actions are constantly guided by him. When we walk in the Lord's presence, everything we see, hear, touch, or taste reminds us of him. That is what is meant by a prayerful life . . . a life in which nothing, absolutely nothing, is done, said, or understood independently of him who is the origin and purpose of our existence.[105]

This is the goal of the uncluttered life. Like all things this side of heaven, uncluttering is not an end in itself, but a means for moving forward as worshipers of God. For this is who God has created us to be. Perhaps it isn't actually about strengthening our core; it's about placing God our rock at our center. Even the greatest six-pack abs on earth can't come close to that.

Conclusion

LIFE, UNCLUTTERED

*Progress. It's good if it doesn't
blind you to what life is all about.
Cut you off from wisdom.*
–Michael D. O'Brien, *Strangers and Sojourners*

How has your uncluttered journey been? It's been a
wild ride for my family and me, to say the least. Some
tears, yes. Euphoria at times, too. But mostly through
the months of this experiment, whether I'm elbow
deep in a junk drawer, working through a budget
spreadsheet, or inviting a new friend in for a visit, I've
been amazed and blessed and awed to experience God
in a thousand small, ordinary ways. Ways I would
have missed if I'd been running at a thousand miles
per hour. Paring down my possessions, simplifying
my schedule, pressing into spiritual disciplines like

silence and tithing (*especially* tithing) have been painful at times. But the pain has done good work. As C. S. Lewis is right to remind us: "Nothing that has not died will be resurrected."[106]

As we've dug down past all the mindless clutter of our lives, we've found the wellspring of life that was there all the while and begun to drink from it with greater regularity, intentionality, and abandon. Poet Scott Cairns quotes Isaac the Syrian who wrote, way back in the seventh century, "The love of God proceeds from our conversing with him; this conversation of prayer comes about through stillness, and stillness arrives with the stripping away of self."[107] Losing the selfish and prideful and arrogant and comfortable pieces of ourselves hasn't been easy, but like most difficult things, it's been *good*. Do I love that I can't walk into a T.J. Maxx without a pang of conviction anymore? Nope. But I love that there's room in my closet for a writing desk, room in my bank account for greater generosity, and room in my schedule for dinner with a neighbor tomorrow and not in three weeks. The sacrifices have hurt—sacrifices always do. But the rewards have been deep and profound and (in many cases) eternal.

You're probably curious: After walking this road as a family for the past year, are we good at all these things all of the time? *Almost* all the time? No, we are not. We are human; we live in America; we have young kids; we get tired and cave on extra stuff, too many events, the occasional digital binge. We swim in the same cultural stew you do—it's hard out there, and temptations abound. Have we somehow "arrived" as perfectly uncluttered people with perfectly peaceful souls? No, we have not. For one thing, our kids are still young, and the challenges of living a life uncluttered shift and change with the ages and stages of our lives. What works with a toddler needs a new translation for an elementary schooler, and yet another new one for a preteen. What worked easily in Wisconsin took some tweaking before it made sense in California. But the major reason we aren't flawlessly following the Christian virtue of simplicity is that sanctification—the process of confessing sin, repenting from it, and little by little becoming more like Jesus—takes time.

There will be more layers of sin and selfishness, clinging and fear that need to come away. I'm a work in progress; Daryl is, too. I think often of the scene from C. S. Lewis's novel, *The Voyage of the Dawn Treader*, where Aslan wants to turn Eustace the dragon back into Eustace the boy. The dragon peels off one layer of skin on his own and then another, but he is still scaly and dragon-y underneath. He can't get all the dragon off of him without help.

"You will have to let me undress you," says Aslan. Eustace, quite frightened but even more desperate to leave his dragonish ways behind, lies down and lets the lion go to work:

> The very first tear he made was so deep that I thought it had gone right into my heart. And when he began pulling the skin off, it hurt worse than anything I've ever felt.
>
> Well, he peeled the beastly stuff right off—just as I thought I'd done it myself the other three times, only they hadn't hurt—and there it was lying on the grass: only ever so much thicker, and darker, and more knobbly-looking than the others had been.... Then he caught hold of me—I didn't like that much for I was very tender underneath now that I'd no skin on—and threw me into the water. It smarted like anything but only for a moment. After that it became perfectly delicious and as soon as I started swimming and splashing I found that all the pain had gone.... I'd turned into a boy again....
>
> After a bit the lion took me out and dressed me ...in new clothes.[108]

The more we peel back the layers of our lives, the more we learn that there is still work to do, that our hearts are deep with caverns of longing and fear, hope and wonder yet to be mined.

Yet this journey has taught me that even the slow, sometimes painful process of sanctification is a very holy one, and admitting to failures and foibles, temptations and trials, is part of the healing process. As Brennan Manning notes in his classic *The Ragamuffin Gospel*, "The mature Christians I have met along the way are those who have failed and have learned to live gracefully within their failure. Faithfulness requires the courage to risk everything on Jesus, the willingness to keep growing, and the readiness to risk failure throughout our lives."[109] One of the risks in writing a book of this kind is that anyone who reads it and comes to visit us will be tempted to look in our drawers, examine our closets, and check out our garage with an eye to the question, "Are they practicing what they preach?" We will never live up to the ideals in this book—let's dispel that illusion right now—but neither will we stop trying. Each small skirmish fought for simplicity will help strengthen us for the next soul battle that lies ahead.

WE WILL NEVER LIVE UP TO THE IDEALS IN THIS BOOK, BUT NEITHER WILL WE STOP TRYING.

It turns out that there are no small things in the economy of God. In our year of uncluttering we've discovered anew that God cares about sparrows and lilies, about toy cars and garages, about calendars and phones, because God cares about us, and each of these things can draw us closer to him or distract us from the work of building his kingdom and the joy of living as his beloved.

While we aren't completely successful each and every moment, we have discovered good and heartening news along the way: it gets easier. It really does! Uncluttering gets quicker and simpler and more effortless because we've begun to develop patterns as a family, hard-won habits that continue to shape us even when we aren't as attentive or intentional as we'd like to be. For example, Lincoln now wakes up on Friday mornings proclaiming, "IT'S SABBATH! WE GET DONUTS!" His delight is a constant reminder to us of the Lord's call to rejoice in his day of rest. The handful of times I've had to work on a Friday, you'd better believe Linc read me the riot act about how God commands me to rest. We've set up direct deposit for our tithes so monthly giving isn't an agonizing decision, it's a matter of course. We never even see that money now—it goes right into the digital offering plate. The longer I live with a simplified closet, the more creatively I use the clothing I already have, and the easier getting dressed is, since I now know each shirt, skirt, and pair of pants by heart.

Our family experiment has inspired friends, family members, and congregants to try their hands at uncluttering, too, and it's been incredibly rewarding to take it on as a communal practice rather than an individual or a family one. My neighbor regularly shares with me stories of her family paring down; a couple in my small group continues to inspire me with their gracious ordering of a God-centered schedule for their kids; my parents aren't buying any new clothes for a year, and they're spending their usual shopping time paring down their closets and selling dishes they no longer use to the online bidders in order to fund a mission trip.

As God slowly and gently continues to open Daryl's and my closed fists, helping us to release control of not only our possessions and our schedule but our very lives to him, we've begun to find deeper and deeper joy in the work he's set before us.

"God is so kind," Daryl said yesterday, coming home after an evening meeting at the church. "God is so kind, and I'm noticing it more and more." Above all, that's what I've learned in this process: to notice. To notice God at work in me and around me; to notice that the hunger of my soul—so easily masked by activity and stuff—is not a desire for any manufactured thing or experience, but a longing for the God of the universe, for the peace and justice and hope and grace that is found only in and through him. I've begun to notice my neighbors, my kids, my family, my friends, my community without the distraction of constant digital connectedness and frenetically running from one activity to the next. To notice creation, nature, the changing of the seasons and the landscape and the weather and the light of each day. To notice, some days, how tired I am and how I ache for the world to be remade anew, without injustice, without cancer, without brokenness, without violence. To notice, on others, how very, very good a world God has made for us and how each ripe strawberry, each mourning dove, each curl in my toddler's hair and caress from my husband's hand and smile from a stranger and word of Scripture and note of music is a pure, magnificent, world-changing gift. As Annie Dillard wrote, "Beauty and grace are performed whether or not we will or sense them. The least we can do is try to be there."[110]

> THE HUNGER OF MY SOUL IS NOT A DESIRE FOR ANY MANUFACTURED THING OR EXPERIENCE, BUT A LONGING FOR THE GOD OF THE UNIVERSE.

God is at work, friends. In you, in me, in our families, in the world. He is here. We are here. Let us notice. And in our newly uncluttered lives, maybe, with his help, we can even take part in this beauty and grace, too.

Acknowledgments

To Dan Balow and the Steve Laube Literary Agency, who believed in me from the start. Dan, you are a gem. I am forever thankful for your encouragement to keep writing. To all the folks at Rose Publishing—especially Lynnette Pennings, who answered all eight million of my questions with wisdom, humor, and grace; and Kay ben-Avraham, whose edits make me sound smarter than I really am.

To Caitlyn and Caroline, with whom I explored the frontiers of kid-clutter back in younger days, and whom I now consider not just sisters but friends.

To my parents, Paul and Barb Belcher, for instilling in me a love of Jesus and literature, even though I'm still a little bit mad you made me put down my novel just because we'd driven 1,200 miles to see Yellowstone.

To my small group, for continually pointing me to Jesus. Your friendship has forever changed me, and your wisdom is all over these pages. And to Maddi, whose awesomeness with kids makes small group possible.

To my writing circles—The Chapter, The Glorious Table, and For the Love. Thank you for your wit, your reminders to keep Jesus at the center, and your willingness to help launch this thing. I love you fiercely, and we are sisters for life.

To my church: Being your pastor is one of my greatest honors and delights. You've taught me so very, very much about hospitality and faith.

To Lincoln and Wilson, the joys of my heart, who grew with this book, and whose sweet gazes and tight hugs remind me daily that real life is worth fighting for and that people are of infinitely more worth than stuff.

And to Daryl, who gave up countless Saturdays, read horrendous first (and second, and third...) drafts, made buckets of coffee, and continues to remind me every step of the way that pursuing a simple, Jesus-centered life is worth everything. I love you more than See's chocolates. And that's saying something.

Bibliography

Armerding, Jake. "The Fleece." In *Walking on the World*. Disc. Compass Records Studio. 2007.

Auden, W. H. "As I Walked Out One Evening." In *Collected Poems*. New York: Vintage Books, 1991.

Augustine. *On Christian Teaching*. Oxford: Oxford University Press, 2008.

Barclay, William. *Matthew*. Vol. 1. Louisville: Westminster, 1970.

Becker, Joshua. "A Helpful Guide to Becoming Unbusy." *Becoming Minimalist*. http://www .becomingminimalist.com/un-busy/.

————. *The More of Less*. Colorado Springs: Waterbrook, 2016.

Belcher, Del. "Cast On Him." In *Cast on Him*. Audiocassette. Brian Basilico Studio. 1984.

Bierce, Ambrose. *The Devil's Dictionary*. New York: Dover Publications, 1993.

Bilton, Nick. "Steve Jobs Was a Low Tech Parent." *The New York Times*. September 10, 2014. https:// www.nytimes.com/2014/09/11/fashion/steve-jobs -apple-was-a-low-tech-parent.html.

Blumhardt, Christopher. "Action in Waiting." In *Watch for the Light: Readings for Advent*. Walden, NY: Plough Publishing, 2001.

The Bob Newhart Show. "Easy for You to Say." Directed by Dick Martin. Written by David Davis, Lorenzo Music, and Andrew Smith. CBS, February 11, 1978.

Bonhoeffer, Dietrich. "Learning to Die." In *A Testament to Freedom: The Essential Writings of Dietrich Bonhoeffer.* Edited by Geffrey B. Kelly and F. Burton Nelson. New York: HarperOne, 1995.

Bosker, Bianca. "The Binge Breaker." *The Atlantic.* November 2016. https://www.theatlantic.com /magazine/archive/2016/11/the-binge-breaker /501122/.

Brown, Brené. *Daring Greatly.* New York: Avery, 2012.

Brueggemann, Walter. *Sabbath as Resistance: Saying No to the Culture of Now.* Louisville: Westminster John Knox, 2014.

Buffett, Warren. Quoted in "Are You Focused Enough?" by Paul B. Brown. *Forbes.* May 10, 2012. http://www.forbes.com/sites /actiontrumpseverything/2012/05/10/are-you -focused-enough-a-surprising-case-study.

Cairns, Scott. *The End of Suffering.* Brewster, MA: Paraclete Press, 2010.

Calhoun, Adele. *The Spiritual Disciplines Handbook.* Downers Grove, IL: InterVarsity Press, 2005.

Calvin, John. *Institutes of the Christian Religion.* Edited by John T. McNeill. Louisville: Westminster Press, 1970.

Carlyle, Thomas. *The Works of Thomas Carlyle.* East Sussex, UK: Delphi Classics, 2015.

Clelland, Jackson. "Why Worry." Sermon, Presbyterian Church of the Master, Mission Viejo, California. August 23, 2015.

Crafton, Barbara Cawthorne. "Living Lent." Pages 15–18 in *Bread and Wine: Readings for Lent and Easter.* Walden, NY: Plough Publishing, 2003.

Crouch, Andy. *The Tech-Wise Family.* Grand Rapids: Baker Books, 2017.

Dawn, Marva. *Keeping the Sabbath Wholly.* Grand Rapids: Eerdmans, 1989.

Dillard, Annie. *Pilgrim at Tinker Creek.* New York: Harper Collins, 1974.

Eisenhower, Dwight D. "Address at the Cow Palace on Accepting the Nomination of the Republican National Convention." August 23, 1956. http://www.presidency.ucsb.edu/ws/index.php?pid=10583.

Eliot, T. S. "Ash Wednesday." In *The Waste Land and Other Poems.* New York: Penguin Classics, 2003.

Elliot, Jim. *The Journals of Jim Elliot.* Edited by Elisabeth Elliot. Grand Rapids: Revell, 1978.

Fields Milburn, Joshua, and Ryan Nicodemus. *The Minimalists.* www.theminimalists.com.

Foster, Brett. *The Garbage Eater.* Evanston, IL: Triquarterly Books/Northwestern University Press, 2011.

Gaffigan, Jim. *Dad Is Fat.* New York: Crown Publishing Group, 2013.

Graham, Billy. *Unto the Hills: A Daily Devotional.* Nashville: Thomas Nelson, 1986.

Greenfield, Susan. *Mind Change.* New York: Random House, 2015.

Heschel, Abraham. *The Sabbath.* New York: Farrar, Straus and Giroux, 1955.

Hughes, Kent. "Giving Now." *Preaching Today,* #205. Carol Stream, IL: Christianity Today International. August 2000. http://www .preachingtoday.com/illustrations/2000 /august/12584.html.

Hugo, Victor. *The Letters of Victor Hugo: From Exile, and After the Fall of the Empire.* New York: Sagwan Press, 2018.

Job, Rueben P., and Norman Shawchuck, eds. *A Guide to Prayer for Ministers and Other Servants.* Nashville: Upper Room Books, 2003.

Keynes, John Maynard. "Economic Possibilities for Our Grandchildren." Pages 17–26 in *Revisiting Keynes: Economic Possibilities for Our Grandchildren.* Edited by Lorenzo Pecci and Gustavo Piga. Cambridge, MA: MIT Press, 2008.

Kreider, Tim. "The 'Busy' Trap." *The New York Times.* June 30, 2012. https://opinionator.blogs.nytimes .com/2012/06/30/the-busy-trap/.

Labberton, Mark. *The Dangerous Act of Worship.* Downers Grove, IL: InterVarsity Press, 2007.

Lamott, Anne. *Traveling Mercies: Some Thoughts on Faith.* New York: Random House, 1999.

Levertov, Denise. "The Depths." In *The Jacob's Ladder.* New York: New Directions, 1958.

Lewis, C. S. *Mere Christianity.* New York: HarperOne, 2015.

———. *The Voyage of the Dawn Treader.* New York: Harper Collins, 1980.

———. *The Weight of Glory.* New York: HarperOne, 2015.

Lewis, Sinclair. *Babbitt.* New York: Dover, 2003.

Manning, Brennan. *The Ragamuffin Gospel.* Sisters, OR: Multnomah, 1990.

Mascolo, Michael. "The Failure of Child-Centered Parenting." *Psychology Today.* May 15, 2015. https://www.psychologytoday.com/us/blog/old -school-parenting-modern-day-families/201505 /the-failure-child-centered-parenting.

McCracken, Brett. *Uncomfortable: The Awkward and Essential Challenge of Christian Community.* Wheaton, IL: Crossway, 2017.

McNeil, Brenda Salter. *Roadmap to Reconciliation: Moving Communities into Unity, Wholeness and Justice.* Downers Grove, IL: InterVarsity Press, 2015.

Melville, Herman. *Bartleby the Scrivener: A Story of Wall Street*. Montgomery, AL: Mockingbird Classics, 2003.

Newman, Elizabeth. *Untamed Hospitality: Welcoming God and Other Strangers*. Grand Rapids: Brazos Press, 2007.

Nouwen, Henri. *The Living Reminder*. New York: Harper Collins, 1977.

Nye, David E. "Critics of Technology." Pages 429–52 in *A Companion to American Technology*. Edited by Carroll Pursell. Malden, MA: Blackwell Publishing, 2008.

O'Brien, Michael D. *Strangers and Sojourners*. San Francisco: Ignatius Press, 1997.

O'Connor, Flannery. Quoted in *Flannery O'Connor: An Introduction* by Miles Orvell. Jackson, MS: University Press of Mississippi, 1991.

Oliver, Mary. "The Summer Day." In *New and Selected Poems*. Vol. 1. Boston: Beacon Press, 1992.

Ortberg, John. *The Life You've Always Wanted*. Grand Rapids: Zondervan, 2002.

Patchett, Ann. "My Year of No Shopping." *The New York Times*. December 17, 2017. https://www.nytimes.com/2017/12/15/opinion/sunday/shopping-consumerism.html.

Perez, Sarah. "US consumers now spend 5 hours per day on mobile devices." *TechCrunch*. March 3, 2017.

https://techcrunch.com/2017/03/03/u-s-consumers
-now-spend-5-hours-per-day-on-mobile-devices/.

Peterson, Eugene. *The Pastor.* New York: HarperOne,
2011.

————. *Tell It Slant: A Conversation on the Language
of Jesus in His Stories and Prayers.* Grand Rapids:
Eerdmans, 2008.

Popescu, Adam. "Keep Your Head Up: How Smartphone
Addiction Kills Manners and Moods." *The New
York Times.* January 25, 2018. https://www
.nytimes.com/2018/01/25/smarter-living
/bad-text-posture-neckpain-mood.html?utm
_source=pocket&utm_medium=email&utm_cam
paign=pockethits&referer=https://getpocket.com/.

Reuters staff. "Bill Gates keeps close eye on kids'
computer time." *Reuters.* February 20, 2007.
https://www.reuters.com/article/us-microsoft
-gates-daughter/bill-gates-keeps-close-eye-on-kids
-computer-time-idUSN2022438420070221.

Taylor, Barbara Brown. *An Altar in the World.* New
York: HarperOne, 2010.

————. *Leaving Church.* New York: HarperOne, 2009.

Thomas á Kempis. *The Imitation of Christ.* Franklin,
TN: Worthy Inspired, 2015.

Tierney, John. "Do You Suffer from Decision Fatigue?"
The New York Times. August 21, 2011. https://
www.nytimes.com/2011/08/21/magazine/do-you
-suffer-from-decision-fatigue.html.

Tugend, Alina. "Too Busy to Notice You're Busy." *The New York Times.* March 31, 2007. https://www.nytimes.com/2007/03/31 /business/31shortcuts.html.

Ward, Benedicta, ed. *The Desert Fathers: Sayings of the Early Christian Monks.* New York: Penguin Classics, 2003.

Warren, Tish Harrison. *Liturgy of the Ordinary.* Downers Grove, IL: InterVarsity Press, 2017.

Weinstein, Victoria. "A Reminder About Fit and Self-Awareness." *Beauty Tips for Ministers.* October 13, 2015. http://beautytipsforministers .com/2015/10/13/a-reminder-about-fit-and-self -awareness/.

"The Westminster Confession." In *The Book of Confessions: The Constitution of the Presbyterian Church (U.S.A.).* Louisville: The Office of the General Assembly, 2014.

Wilder, Laura Ingalls. *Little House in the Big Woods.* New York: Harper Collins, 2004.

Wright, N. T. *The Way of the Lord: Christian Pilgrimage Today.* Grand Rapids: Eerdmans, 1999.

Yancey, Philip. "The death of reading is threatening the soul." *The Washington Post.* July 21, 2017. https://www.washingtonpost.com/news/acts -of-faith/wp/2017/07/21/the-death-of-reading -is-threatening-the-soul/?noredirect=on&utm _term=.2f5b011fe2a6.

Notes

Chapter 2: Stuff

1 John Ortberg, *The Life You've Always Wanted* (Grand Rapids: Zondervan, 2002), 128.

2 Barbara Cawthorne Crafton, "Living Lent," in *Bread and Wine: Readings for Lent and Easter* (Walden, NY: Plough Publishing, 2003), 18.

3 Matt. 6:20–21.

4 Joshua Fields Milburn and Ryan Nicodemus, "Just in Case," *The Minimalists*, https://www.theminimalists.com/jic/.

Chapter 3: Clothing

5 John Tierney, "Do You Suffer from Decision Fatigue?," *The New York Times*, August 21, 2011, https://www.nytimes.com/2011/08/21/magazine/do-you-suffer-from-decision-fatigue.html.

6 1 Pet. 3:3.

7 1 Sam. 16:7.

8 Victoria Weinstein, "A Reminder About Fit and Self-Awareness," *Beauty Tips for Ministers*, October 13, 2015, http://beautytipsforministers.com/2015/10/13/a-reminder-about-fit-and-self-awareness/.

Chapter 4: New Stuff

9 Ann Patchett, "My Year of No Shopping," *The New York Times*, December 17, 2017, https://www.nytimes.com/2017/12/15/opinion/sunday/shopping-consumerism.html (emphasis mine).

10 Syncletica, in *The Desert Fathers: Sayings of the Early Christian Monks*, ed. Benedicta Ward (New York: Penguin Classics, 2003), 105.

11 *The Bob Newhart Show*, "Easy for You to Say," CBS, February 11, 1978, written by David Davis, Lorenzo Music, and Andrew Smith, directed by Dick Martin.

12 Isa. 55:1–2.

13 Rev. 21:5.

14 Anne Lamott, *Traveling Mercies: Some Thoughts on Faith* (New York: Random House, 1999), 196.

15 C. S. Lewis, *Mere Christianity* (New York: HarperOne, 2015), 138.

Chapter 5: Technology

16 Thomas Carlyle, *The Works of Thomas Carlyle* (East Sussex, UK: Delphi Classics, 2015), 183.

17 Ambrose Bierce, "Telephone," *The Devil's Dictionary* (New York: Dover Publications, 1993), 124.

18 Susan Greenfield, *Mind Change* (New York: Random House, 2015), 17.

19 Ibid., 19.

20 Sarah Perez, "US consumers now spend 5 hours per day on mobile devices," *TechCrunch*, March 3, 2017, https://techcrunch.com/2017/03/03/u-s-consumers-now-spend-5-hours-per-day-on-mobile-devices/.

21 Mary Oliver, "The Summer Day" in *New and Selected Poems*, Vol. 1 (Boston: Beacon Press, 1992), 94.

22 Philip Yancey, "The death of reading is threatening the soul," *The Washington Post*, July 21, 2017, https://www.washingtonpost.com/news/acts-of-faith/wp/2017/07/21/the-death-of-reading-is-threatening-the-soul/?noredirect=on&utm_term=.2f5b011fe2a6.

23 Andy Crouch, *The Tech-Wise Family* (Grand Rapids: Baker Books, 2017), 26–27.

24 Bianca Bosker, "The Binge Breaker," *The Atlantic Monthly*, November 2016, https://www.theatlantic.com/magazine/archive/2016/11/the-binge-breaker/501122/.

25 John Calvin, *Institutes of the Christian Religion*, ed. John T. McNeill (Louisville: Westminster Press, 1970), 2.2.8.

26 Yancey, "The death of reading."

27 Gal. 5:1.

Chapter 6: Schedule

28 Herman Melville, *Bartleby the Scrivener: A Story of Wall Street* (Montgomery, AL: Mockingbird Classics, 2003), 19–23.

29 Brené Brown, Twitter post, December 21, 2010, https://twitter
.com/brenebrown/status/33648241232977920.

30 Joshua Becker, "A Helpful Guide to Becoming Unbusy,"
Becoming Minimalist, http://www.becomingminimalist.com
/un-busy/.

31 Tim Kreider, "The 'Busy' Trap," *The New York Times*, June 30,
2012, https://opinionator.blogs.nytimes.com/2012/06/30/the
-busy-trap/.

32 John Maynard Keynes, "Economic Possibilities for Our
Grandchildren," in *Revisiting Keynes: Economic Possibilities
for Our Grandchildren*, ed. Lorenzo Pecchi and Gustavo Piga
(Cambridge, MA: MIT Press, 2008), 25.

33 David E. Nye, "Critics of Technology," in *A Companion to
American Technology*, ed. Carroll Pursell (Malden, MA:
Blackwell Publishing, 2008), 429–52.

34 Dwight D. Eisenhower, "Address at the Cow Palace on
Accepting the Nomination of the Republican National
Convention," August 23, 1956. http://www.presidency.ucsb
.edu/ws/index.php?pid=10583. (Also, can we all just pause for a
moment and appreciate that this address happened at someplace
called The COW PALACE? A place that, by the way, still exists?
Google it.)

35 Ben Hunnicutt, quoted in Brigid Schulte, "Why Being Too Busy
Makes Us Feel Good," in *The Washington Post*, March 14,
2014, https://www.washingtonpost.com/opinions/why-being
-too-busy-makes-us-feel-so-good/2014/03/14/c098f6c8-9e81
-11e3-a050-dc3322a94fa7_story.html?noredirect=on&utm
_term=.dbc664399aed.

36 Rom. 1:22–23.

37 Victor Hugo, *The Letters of Victor Hugo: From Exile, and After
the Fall of the Empire* (New York: Sagwan Press, 2018), 23.

Chapter 7: The Secret of Simplicity

38 1 Cor. 10:14.

39 1 Pet. 4:3.

40 Brett McCracken, *Uncomfortable: The Awkward and Essential
Challenge of Christian Community* (Wheaton, IL: Crossway,
2017), 151.

41   Barbara Brown Taylor, *Leaving Church* (New York: HarperOne, 2009), 175.

42   Ibid., 230.

43   Jim Gaffigan, *Dad Is Fat* (New York: Crown Publishing Group, 2013), 186.

44   Lewis, *Mere Christianity*, 206.

45   Eugene Peterson, *Tell It Slant: A Conversation on the Language of Jesus in His Stories and Prayers* (Grand Rapids: Eerdmans, 2008), 70.

46   Luke 13:19.

47   Matt. 6:25–26.

48   Matt. 6:31–33.

49   Lamott, *Traveling Mercies*, 82.

50   Luke 14:27.

51   1 Pet. 3:14.

Chapter 8: Sabbath

52   Eugene Peterson, *The Pastor* (New York: HarperOne, 2011), 220.

53   Walter Brueggemann, *Sabbath as Resistance: Saying No to the Culture of Now* (Louisville: Westminster John Knox, 2014), 19.

54   1 John 5:3 (ESV).

55   Anne Lamott's Facebook page, April 8, 2015, https://www.facebook.com/AnneLamott/posts/662177577245222.

56   Laura Ingalls Wilder, *Little House in the Big Woods* (New York: Harper Collins, 2004), 85.

57   Abraham Heschel, *The Sabbath* (New York: Farrar, Straus and Giroux, 1955), 14.

58   Brueggemann, *Sabbath as Resistance*, 40–41.

59   Adele Calhoun, *The Spiritual Disciplines Handbook* (Downers Grove, IL: InterVarsity Press, 2005), 43.

60   Heschel, *The Sabbath*, 20.

61   Susannah Heschel, foreword to *The Sabbath*, by Abraham Heschel, vii.

62   Kreider, "The 'Busy' Trap."

63 Barbara Brown Taylor, *An Altar in the World* (New York: HarperOne, 2010), 136.

64 Marva Dawn, *Keeping the Sabbath Wholly* (Grand Rapids: Eerdmans, 1989), 61.

Chapter 9: Hospitality

65 Lev. 19:33–34.

66 Elizabeth Newman, *Untamed Hospitality: Welcoming God and Other Strangers* (Grand Rapids: Brazos Press, 2007), 181.

67 Luke 14:13–14.

68 1 Pet. 4:9.

69 Rom. 12:3.

70 Newman, *Untamed Hospitality*, 174.

71 John 12:13.

72 Luke 19:1–10.

73 Acts 20:35.

74 Luke 10:42 (MSG).

Chapter 10: Listening and Speaking

75 1 Kings 19:4.

76 1 Kings 19:11–13.

77 N. T. Wright, *The Way of the Lord: Christian Pilgrimage Today* (Grand Rapids: Eerdmans, 1999), 4.

78 Tish Harrison Warren, *Liturgy of the Ordinary* (Downers Grove, IL: InterVarsity Press, 2017), 112.

79 T. S. Eliot, "Ash Wednesday," in *The Waste Land and Other Poems* (New York: Penguin Classics, 2003), 76.

80 1 Thess. 5:17.

81 James 5:13.

Chapter 11: Uncluttered Kids

82 Matt. 10:37.

83 Michael Mascolo, "The Failure of Child-Centered Parenting," *Psychology Today*, May 15, 2015, https://www.psychologytoday.com/blog/old-school-parenting-modern-day-families/201505/the-failure-child-centered-parenting.

84 Matt. 19:14.

85 Crouch, *The Tech-Wise Family*, 191.

86 Ginger Newingham's Facebook page, accessed September 25, 2017, https://www.facebook.com/gingernewingham/grid?lst=20 009563%3A1377003285%3A1524452027.

87 "Bill Gates keeps close eye on kids' computer time," *Reuters*, February 20, 2007, https://www.reuters.com/article/us -microsoft-gates-daughter/bill-gates-keeps-close-eye-on-kids -computer-time-idUSN2022438420070221.

88 Nick Bilton, "Steve Jobs Was a Low Tech Parent," *The New York Times*, September 10, 2014, https://www.nytimes .com/2014/09/11/fashion/steve-jobs-apple-was-a-low-tech -parent.html.

89 Adam Popescu, "Keep Your Head Up: How Smartphone Addiction Kills Manners and Moods," *The New York Times*, January 25, 2018, https://www.nytimes.com/2018/01/25 /smarter-living/bad-text-posture-neckpain-mood.html?utm _source=pocket&utm_medium=email&utm_campaign =pockethits&referer=https://getpocket.com/.

Chapter 12: Generosity

90 Kent Hughes, "Giving Now," *Preaching Today*, #205 (Carol Stream, IL: Christianity Today International), August 2000, http://www.preachingtoday.com/illustrations/2000 /august/12584.html.

91 Ps. 50:10.

92 Brené Brown, *Daring Greatly* (New York: Avery, 2012), 29 (emphasis mine).

93 Del Belcher, "Cast on Him" in *Cast on Him*, Brian Basilico Studio, 1984, audiocassette.

94 J. D. Rockefeller. The quote may be apocryphal. Another version of the story notes him as saying, "Just one more dollar."

95 Mal. 3:8–10 (emphasis mine).

96 Col. 1:16.

Chapter 13: Worship

97 Mark Labberton, *The Dangerous Act of Worship* (Downers Grove, IL: InterVarsity Press, 2007), 25–26.

98 "The Westminster Confession," in *The Book of Confessions: The Constitution of the Presbyterian Church (U.S.A)* (Louisville: The Office of the General Assembly, 2014), gender inclusive language mine.

99 Labberton, *The Dangerous Act of Worship*, 44.

100 William Barclay, *Matthew*, vol. 1 (Louisville: Westminster, 1970), 386.

101 Jim Elliot, *The Journals of Jim Elliot*, ed. Elisabeth Elliot (Grand Rapids: Revell, 1978), 174.

102 Dietrich Bonhoeffer, "Learning to Die," in *A Testament to Freedom: The Essential Writings of Dietrich Bonhoeffer*, ed. Geffrey B. Kelly and F. Burton Nelson (New York: HarperOne, 1995), 268.

103 Carlo Carretto, *The God Who Comes* (Maryknoll, NY: Orbis Books, 1974), quoted in *A Guide to Prayer for Ministers and Other Servants*, ed. Rueben P. Job and Norman Shawchuck (Nashville: Upper Room Books, 2003), 174.

104 Ps. 36:9.

105 Henri Nouwen, *The Living Reminder* (New York: Harper Collins, 1977), 28.

Chapter 14: Conclusion

106 C. S. Lewis, *The Weight of Glory* (New York: HarperOne, 2015), 173.

107 Scott Cairns, *The End of Suffering* (Brewster, MA: Paraclete Press, 2010), 11.

108 C. S. Lewis, *The Voyage of the Dawn Treader* (New York: Harper Collins, 1980), 86–87.

109 Brennan Manning, *The Ragamuffin Gospel* (Sisters, OR: Multnomah, 1990), 185.

110 Annie Dillard, *Pilgrim at Tinker Creek* (New York: Harper Collins, 1974), 10.